MEN
OF POWER

A BOOK OF DICTATORS

By Albert Carr

ILLUSTRATIONS BY MARC SIMONT

THE VIKING PRESS · NEW YORK
1940

FIRST PUBLISHED SEPTEMBER 1940

An Open Letter

TO JOEL CARR

DEAR JOEL:

Not long ago you asked me a question that took me by surprise. You said, "What good does it do to read history?" It was such a big, serious question that I did not care to answer it offhand; but this is a good time and place to get at it.

Think of yourself as an explorer in, let us say, Central Asia. You are about to cross a great range of mountains where there are strange and possibly unfriendly tribes. What do you do—sling a pack over your shoulder and start climbing without another thought? I hope not. Explorers who stake their lives on their ability to master the unknown cannot afford to be impulsive. If you are wise, you will make careful preparations. You will find out what you can about the customs and language of the tribes ahead, read the reports of previous explorers, provide yourself with warm clothing, food, maps, compasses, and gifts for the tribal chieftains. When you have done all that and more, then you set out.

Now in a very real sense you are an explorer, and so am I, so is everyone. But instead of exploring countries, we are exploring *time*. Instead of making our journey in geography, we are, so to speak, making it in history. The things that we do, and that our nation does, from day to day and from year to year become part of the great story of mankind—just as the mountains and rivers that our Asiatic explorer discovers become part of geography.

Like the explorer, we do not know exactly what we are going to find, or what is going to happen to us on our journey through the future. Will there be wars, revolutions, hard times? If so, it would certainly seem wiser to make some preparations now, rather than shut our eyes and plunge blindly ahead. As sensible people, then, we want to try to guess the dangers that lie before us so that they will not take us by surprise.

Of course we know that no one can predict exactly what will happen. We must have an explorer's courage to meet the unexpected. But we can go a long way to increase our chances of success in exploring the future if we have a clear idea of what is going on in the world at present, and if we know what other "explorers," in similar circumstances, have found in the past.

To get information about the present we read newspapers, and listen to the radio, and in other ways inform ourselves about "current events." And to learn what the past can tell us, we turn to the record of the important happenings in man's journey through time—the record which we call history.

Reading this record of past centuries, one often comes across a passage that makes one say, "Well, but something like that seems to be happening right here. Let me read on, and find out how things turned out back there, hundreds of years ago. Because if they made a mistake then, it's possible that we're making a mistake now." In this way history can help us avoid disaster. It can be a kind of chart and compass for civilized men to use in guiding themselves into the future with as little pain and trouble as possible.

Of course, it is of the utmost importance that the statesmen who lead a nation and make its laws should know history. And it is desirable, too, that every intelligent citizen should be able to think for himself about the way things are going in the world, and in his country, so that he can vote for good men and good causes in elections. But there is another and more personal reason why history should interest you.

A knowledge of history helps a man to become a leader in whatever he undertakes. The leaders in all walks of life must know how men think and feel—what makes them act—what they will work for and fight for. And history is really an account of how men have thought and felt and worked and fought through the ages.

Both as a citizen of a great nation, and as a private person, you will find the lessons of history useful all your life.

ALBERT CARR

New York, N. Y.
Feb. 1, 1940.

Acknowledgments

I wish to express my thanks to several young people whose thoughtful criticisms and suggestions aided me in preparing this book—especially to Nellie Robinson and Richard Seaton of Woodstock, N. Y., and to Barbara Johnson and Richard Johnson of Bronxville, N. Y.

※

Foreword

Power! It is a magic word. No moment in history is more exciting than when a lone figure leaps suddenly into the saddle and waves his sword above the crowd. The true story of the men of power is more astonishing than any fairy tale. How does it happen that a single man, often of humble birth, obtains control over the lives and happiness of many millions of his people? What is there about him that makes ordinary men bow before him, so that by a word he can change the fate of his whole country? What mysterious force enables the Cromwells and Napoleons and Hitlers to stride ruthlessly across the stage of human history, building, changing, and destroying almost at will?

This book will, I hope, help you to answer these questions for yourself. But it has another purpose, too. We live at a time when the men of power, whom we call dictators, are reaching out to touch the lives of all of us, even in free countries like our own. No doubt you know something about Hitler, Stalin, and Mussolini, and something about the dictators who have gone before them. But it is not enough just to know something. As the years go by, you may hear people say, as some were saying not long ago, that we in America would be wise to get rid of our Congress and have a dictator. You may hear them say that the kind of government we have now is out of date. You may hear them say that democracy is getting us into trouble, and that when Abraham Lincoln spoke of "government of the people, by the people, for the people," he was talking nonsense.

If such a time comes, you will want to be able to form your own opinion. You will want to know what dictatorship is all about; why it appeals so strongly to people in other countries—people very much like us. You will want to know what these dictators—these men of power—stand for. You will want to be able to measure for yourself the good or harm that they have done.

And you will be helped in deciding what your own country ought to do about its government if you remember that there have been a great many dictators in other times and places, for thousands of years past. In ancient Egypt and Greece and Rome and China, there were men of power so much like Hitler, Mussolini, and Company that the similarity takes your breath away. Here in this book, however, we will not go so far back. In relatively recent times there have been many strong men whose stories are more useful in aiding us to understand the world around us than the career of a Julius Caesar or an Alexander the Great. So we will confine ourselves to men who rose to fame and power in the last three hundred years or thereabouts—men whose deeds, for good or evil, were so tremendous that we cannot read of them without amazement.

A. C.

Contents

RICHELIEU MOLDS A NATION   17

CROMWELL LEADS A REVOLUTION   47

FREDERICK FALLS IN LOVE WITH WAR   73

NAPOLEON TRIES TO CONQUER EUROPE   95

BOLÍVAR FIGHTS FOR FREEDOM   123

BISMARCK BUILDS AN EMPIRE   149

MUSSOLINI STRIKES AGAINST DEMOCRACY   179

STALIN MASTERS THE SOVIETS   207

HITLER CHALLENGES THE WEST   237

ABOUT POWER AND DEMOCRACY   269

Richelieu

Richelieu Molds a Nation

O N a spring day in the year 1597, a dusty carriage drawn
by two sturdy horses entered the south gate of the city
of Paris, and began to clatter over the cobbled streets.
The coat of arms on the door and the coachman's faded livery
suggested that the otherwise ordinary carriage belonged to some
minor nobleman. Within there were only a twelve-year-old boy,
looking eagerly around him, and a gray-haired lackey, half
asleep. The well-fed shopkeepers and busy artisans and tattered
loungers who saw them go by paid little attention. There was no
fortune-teller to prophesy that the boy who stared so intently out
of the carriage window would one day be the master of France,
more powerful even than the King—a man whose name would
be uttered in whispered fear and awe.

Through the teeming city the carriage went on its jolting way
to a house not far from the King's great palace. There the old
lackey got out and spoke to a servant who came to the door. Was
Monsieur de Richelieu at home? Then please to inform him that
his brother had arrived.

BOYHOOD OF A FUTURE DICTATOR

It was in this way that young Armand du Plessis, of the noble
house of Richelieu, first came to Paris for a gentleman's educa-

tion, as had his brothers before him. In those days, ordinary people received little schooling unless they happened to be exceptionally ambitious or gifted. For the most part only the families of nobles and well-to-do commoners learned even to read and write. During early childhood, these favorites of fortune might attend a Latin school or be tutored privately by some priest. Thereafter, if they were intelligent, the sons might go directly to one of the great universities.

So it was that Armand, at the age of twelve, was received into the famous University of Paris. There he made rapid progress. A quick and thorough student, he learned to speak Latin with ease, became familiar with Greek, Roman, and French history, and was filled with a deep respect for literature. Later he was to master the Italian and Spanish tongues. You will find, as you read about great statesmen, that most of them could speak other languages than their own; and that this ability was of great importance to them in their rise to power.

At that time, a young nobleman who wanted a career had either to become a soldier or to enter the Church. To practice a profession like the law or medicine, or to learn a trade, was simply unheard of for the "well-born." There was actually a law which said that a nobleman who lowered himself so far as to command a merchant vessel must forfeit his titles.

Of course, if a young man or woman had good connections at the court, he (or she) might become a courtier, in attendance on the royal family. Armand's older brother, Henri, for example, was made a "Gentleman of the Chamber," and received a pension, or salary, which in our money would come to about $10,000 a year. This large sum came from the King's treasury—that is, from money paid by the common people in taxes. To earn it,

Henri had to do little except have good manners, and please the King and the royal family by his cleverness, good looks, and fashionable clothes.

Madame de Richelieu, Armand's mother, decided that since Henri was provided for, her second son, Alphonse, should go into the Church, while Armand, the youngest, became a soldier. So at the age of eighteen, Armand left the University to enter a fashionable military school. Here he became an expert in horsemanship and swordplay, and studied military history and strategy.

FROM SOLDIER TO BISHOP

But about this time, a curious thing happened that completely changed the plan of Armand's life. As you are perhaps aware, people in Richelieu's time were not in the least proud about accepting money and other gifts from the royal family and the great nobles. Contemptible as it may seem to us today, it was quite usual then for an otherwise respectable man to flatter and bribe the King's ministers and favorites until they obtained a pension for him, or a grant of lands, or some easy job with a big salary. Madame de Richelieu wrote to the King of France, Henri IV, and told him how grateful she was for his kindness to her son Henri, and discreetly reminded him that her second son, Alphonse—Armand's older brother—was growing up and had religious inclinations. The King, remembering that the boy's father had been a good friend and loyal soldier, was quite willing to do something more for the family. So he proposed to make Alphonse a bishop, and to give him a bishopric, or diocese, to govern. Of course, the Pope in Rome had to approve the appointment, but that was considered largely a matter of form.

To everyone's surprise, brother Alphonse objected. A bishop had serious responsibilities to Church and Crown. For one thing, he had to collect taxes and divide them with Rome and the King. Alphonse preferred to enter a religious order as a monk, so that he could devote himself entirely to spiritual affairs.

His mother did not oppose him. But she wanted to make sure that the bishopric remained in the family. Would it not be possible, she suggested to the King, to nominate Armand as the bishop, instead of Alphonse? The King agreed.

Whereupon Armand, just twenty years old, and about to become an officer in the army, suddenly found himself a bishop-to-be. He did not object in the least, for he had a wholesome respect for money; in time he became the wealthiest man in France. True, the diocese of Luçon, to which he had been nominated, was small and poor. Nevertheless, it brought in a sum equal to about $50,000 a year, out of which he might be able to hold on to $12,000 for himself.

Then a difficulty arose. It was a rule of the Church that a man had to be twenty-five years old before he could be consecrated as a bishop. Months went by, yet no word came from the Pope confirming young Richelieu's appointment. Finally Henri IV suggested that Armand go to Rome and try to persuade the Pope to make an exception in his favor.

Richelieu went. In Rome he found that the Pope was surrounded by shrewd Italian politicians, some of whom would do nothing without a bribe, while others were sternly opposed to Armand's request. Now for the first time it became clear what sort of man Richelieu had grown to be. After careful study of the situation, he cautiously "made a gift" to a certain influential politician. Then he forged his birth certificate so as to appear five years older than he was. Thereafter he obtained an audience with the Pope.

Even now he was uneasy lest the Pope see through the forgery, so he determined to make him overlook the little matter of age. Shortly before the audience was to take place, Richelieu attended a church service at which the Pope was also present. There a priest delivered a powerful sermon. Richelieu had a fine memory, and he listened carefully. A little later he was ushered into the Pope's presence, and made a great impression by repeating, word for word, the sermon to which they had both listened a little earlier.

Some people think that Richelieu had secretly got hold of a copy of the sermon in advance, and had plenty of time to memorize it. Possibly the Pope thought so too, because he is supposed to have smiled and said, "This young man has all the promise of a great knave." However, he granted Richelieu's desire, and made him Bishop of Luçon.

THE LOVE FOR POWER REVEALS ITSELF

This tale of Richelieu in Rome is not very important as history, but it is important for what it tells us about his character. Already he was cold, clever, calculating, unscrupulous, and bold. Furthermore, he was tremendously ambitious. He wanted to become powerful at court and in France. And he laid his plans accordingly.

If he had wished, he could have stayed in Paris most of the time, as many churchmen did, living on the income from his bishopric, while others attended to his duties. But he was not interested in a soft life. After paying his respects to the King, he journeyed to his little diocese of Luçon, and went energetically to work.

Energy is something that every successful man has in abundance. Richelieu's energy for work was remarkable. He would stay at his desk for twenty hours a day if necessary, dictating letters, talking with men of affairs, reading and writing reports. Under his rule the diocese soon began to prosper. The people approved of their bishop, for although he was severe, he was also just.

Influential men began to take notice of Richelieu, for he was in the habit of writing letters to everybody of importance. One of the most powerful churchmen of France said of him, "Men do not put themselves to such pains without some great purpose in view." But although Richelieu liked to advertise himself, he was very careful how he did it. To avoid mistakes he wrote out a series of "rules of conduct"—rules which are still sound for people who want to get on in the world. Never appear anxious for favors, he told himself. Never fish for invitations. Never boast. Always make sure your conversation is interesting, but avoid gossip and harsh remarks about others. And most important of all, never leave to chance what can be achieved by calculation.

RICHELIEU SHOWS HIS PATIENCE

In the year 1610, when Richelieu was twenty-five, the sudden news came that King Henri IV had been assassinated. Richelieu spent no time in regrets. At once he began to scheme how this sad event might be turned to advantage. He wanted to become a minister of France. Obviously, then, he had to gain the good will of the widowed Queen Marie, who would be Regent of France until her son Louis came of age.

Richelieu wrote a flowery letter of condolence to the Queen, and sent it to his courtier brother Henri, asking him to deliver it in person. Henri refused. The letter, he said, struck him as pushing and vulgar. Another man than Richelieu might have become angry. But he was far too wise to refuse advice when it had good sense behind it. He destroyed the letter, and turned to another method of reaching the Queen's ear.

Among his friends was a certain monk, Father Joseph, a man of noble birth, who was an adviser to several powerful families. Father Joseph recognized the young bishop's talents, and determined to aid him. In later years, when Richelieu was dictator of France, the monk became his chief assistant and head of his spy system; and the two were known as the "Red Cardinal" and the "Gray Cardinal." Through Father Joseph, after the King's murder, Richelieu was able to send the Queen a "confidential report" on political matters, a shrewd document. She liked it, and consented to receive him at court.

Although Richelieu was not exactly handsome, nevertheless his thin face, with its fierce, lustrous eyes and hawk-like nose, commanded respect from everyone; and he spoke eloquently and sensibly. Still, the Queen showed no intention of doing anything for him. Richelieu went back to Luçon. He continued, however, to send letters and reports to the court. His patience and persistence when he had a purpose in view were boundless.

Five years went by in this way. And then, all at once, he sprang into fame.

FRANCE IS TORN

France, in the early 1600's, was a country filled with unrest. In the first place, the great religious wars of Europe between Catholics and Protestants had set Frenchman against Frenchman. The large majority of the people were Catholics, but some important noblemen, and many of the successful business men, were of the Protestant faith. Under King Henri IV, himself a Protestant, the quarrel had been eased; but after his death, it once more became acute.

Closely linked to this cause of trouble was another. Trade had been growing rapidly in France for a century. Merchants and men of business generally were making more money than ever before. But they were not making as much as they might have, because of the tax laws of the country; and they were demanding that the laws be changed.

The word "taxes" does not sound exciting, but a great deal of the trouble and many of the wars of the world have come to pass because people could not agree who was to pay taxes, and how much, and to whom. So it was in France when Marie was Queen. If you really want to get at the heart of these times, you must first understand the struggle which was going on over money.

Under the old feudal laws, the King was not by any means all-powerful in France. The great dukes regarded themselves as nearly equal to him in importance. The country was really a loosely united group of dukedoms with a king at the head to keep peace among them and lead them to war against enemies.

Each important nobleman had the right to make the peasants who lived on his lands and the tradesmen in his towns pay him a

large part of their crops and earnings as taxes. But the great
nobles themselves did not have to pay taxes to the King. The King
got most of his money from his personal estates, and from a tax
on salt.

Presently the King found that he could not rule France properly unless he had more money. He wanted to collect taxes from
peasants and towns all over France. But some of the great nobles
said, in effect, "No, you don't! You can't tax my people. If there's
any more taxing to be done, I'll do it."

This was a cause of trouble between the throne and the dukes.
In this dispute many business men were on the side of the
throne, for they were tired of paying big taxes to the feudal lords.
Furthermore, they were frequently bullied and robbed by the
troops of the nobles. Many of them began to ask the King to protect them against their local lords.

To make the tangle worse, after King Henri IV died, Queen
Marie was very much under the influence of a certain handsome
Italian named Concini, who was hated by most of the French. A
little group of hangers-on had formed around him, and were getting the benefit of the royal pensions and gifts of land. Many families which had formerly shared in these gifts considered themselves cheated, and so were bitter against the court.

Of course, none of these people, neither the Queen, nor nobles,
nor lawyers, nor great merchants, ever gave much thought to the
real source of the wealth they squabbled over. The peasant and
the serf, sweating at the plow and tending the cattle on the estates of richer men, the blacksmiths, wheelwrights, and tanners,
the masons and carpenters, the shepherds and weavers, and the
little shopkeepers of France—these were forgotten men. They
grew the grain and made the goods that others sold, they paid

the bulk of the taxes to nobles, Crown and Church, they made possible the gorgeous palace of Monseigneur, and the diamond necklace of Madame la Duchesse. But aside from the right to work, they had no rights worth mentioning under feudal law. In the eyes of their masters, the poor were on earth to serve the rich; and those who dared say otherwise were dangerous men.

RICHELIEU TASTES POWER

Largely because of quarrels over money, a group of restless dukes were threatening to rebel against Marie and Concini. To keep them quiet, the Queen began to pay them enormous sums —out of the people's taxes, of course. Naturally, when the nobles found she could be bullied in this way, they did it again and again. Finally the time came when the treasury was empty. Then the rebellious lords changed their song. They demanded that Marie call a meeting of the French parliament, known as the States General.

The States General took its name from the so-called "Three Estates" of France—the nobility, the clergy, and the untitled owners of property. The many millions of people who had no property were not represented. Under French tradition, the States General was a highly respected body, and when it expressed an opinion, the throne usually had to give heed. But it could not meet except at the royal command, and naturally the proud kings of France had no wish to be hampered by criticism from their subjects. So they called the States General together only when they were absolutely forced to do so. Marie had little choice.

Although many of the members of this parliament were entitled to sit in it because of their noble birth, others were elected, and still others were appointed by the throne. In his quiet way, Father Joseph saw to it that when the States General met in Paris, Richelieu sat among the representatives of the clergy.

From the beginning, the nobles attacked the Crown violently, demanding the dismissal of Concini and various legal reforms. For a while it looked as if the Queen would have either to meet their demands, or face civil war. Then, when the quarrel was at its hottest, Richelieu rose to speak.

Now his brilliance in politics was revealed. Of course most of his speech was taken up with the reasons why all the Estates should give unquestioning loyalty to the Queen, whom he flattered in the exaggerated way that was then customary. At the same time, however, he managed to confuse the actual problems which were being discussed until neither the nobles nor the merchants and lawyers were quite sure what they wanted. The effect of his eloquent oration was to make the Queen's enemies hesitate, and to enable her to dissolve the States General without having to give way on any important point.

Marie was delighted. To show her appreciation she obtained for Richelieu the post of financial agent for her daughter, who was the Queen of Spain. This gave him a chance to learn the ways in which royalty raised money when it ran short, and also to make a considerable amount for himself. After a brief time the Queen of Spain gave such a glowing report of his abilities that Marie decided to use him in her own service.

First she sent him to talk with the still rebellious dukes. Again he did well. And then at last, in the year 1616, a really important opportunity came his way. The position of Secretary for Foreign Affairs in the high Council of State became open, and the Queen selected Richelieu to fill it. In this way, although he was only thirty-one years old, he became one of the leading ministers of France.

RICHELIEU OPPOSES ROME

In the councils of state, the Queen and Concini listened to Richelieu with respect. Not only did he have definite ideas about what ought to be done, but in addition he was able to explain his ideas in the straightforward, logical way that appeals to the French mind. First of all, he said, let us stop bribing these disloyal dukes. There is only one way to deal with them—by force. And he won consent to denounce the dukes as rebels and to send three armies against them.

Then he took a bolder step. In those days, the Catholic Church was very powerful in French politics. One of the strong ideas of the Church—and an idea with which many great non-Catholic thinkers agree—is that a man's religious faith, the way he lives and feels about life, is far more important than his allegiance to any king or country. While this idea was generally accepted, Rome was able to control the kings of Europe. The most powerful country in Europe, the Holy Roman Empire, was pledged to serve the Catholic religion. The Habsburgs, rulers of the Empire, were masters of Austria, part of Germany, Spain, and the Netherlands—and they were devoting all their might to fighting the Protestants of Germany and Flanders.

Richelieu, in the pursuit of his own ambitions, wanted to make France stronger than any other country. But before that could be done, he would have to defeat the Empire; and before he could defeat the Empire, it would be necessary to unite all Frenchmen behind the throne. Catholic and Protestant, nobleman, priest, merchant, and peasant—all would have to stop fighting each other and obey their royal ruler before the armies of France could make Europe tremble.

Richelieu held that French Catholics could no longer allow their loyalty to Rome to conflict with their loyalty to the throne. Religious obedience must give way to patriotism. These were very startling ideas for that time, particularly in a bishop. But Richelieu had so much confidence in himself that he did not hesitate to express them. He told the Queen: It is not the Protestants who are our enemy, it is Spain. A French Protestant is more precious to France than a Spanish Catholic.

Marie was a devout Catholic. She did not quite like all this talk against the interests of Rome. But she was desperately anxious to raise more money. And she saw that the only way she could persuade her unhappy people to pay larger taxes to the Crown was by uniting the country as Richelieu suggested. So she gave the young statesman a chance to show what he could do.

EXILE

Rome and all Europe were greatly agitated by this sudden explosion of "nationalistic" ideas in Paris. Richelieu began to be talked of everywhere. And then, suddenly, came misfortune—something that he had not foreseen.

Concini, the hated Italian, was stabbed to death, and a powerful clique of nobles demanded that the Queen give up her powers as Regent of France. They persuaded her son, Louis XIII, then sixteen years old, to claim his royal rights and banish his mother from Paris, for he had always resented her affection for Concini. Young as he was, therefore, Louis took command of the government, and as his chief minister appointed a nobleman named Luynes, who had really planned the entire conspiracy.

As the friend of Concini and Marie, Richelieu was disliked by Luynes. Yet he was not a man to be lightly pushed aside. Punctually he attended the first meeting of the Council of State under Louis. At the door he was stopped. One of Luynes's men asked him, "Under what title do you come?"

Richelieu's talents were known and his judgment was valued. If he had said, "As councilor," he could probably have remained, a subordinate to Luynes. But Richelieu was too proud a man to be subordinate to anybody. "I come as minister of the Crown!" he replied haughtily. After that, of course, they forbade him entry, for Luynes was not going to have any ministers whom he did not appoint himself.

Although startled by this sudden fall from power, Richelieu was not at all crushed. Marie had gone to live in southern France, and Richelieu determined to follow her. He made this decision appear a noble gesture on his part, but actually it was as coldly calculated as all his actions. He knew that sooner or later he would be banished anyhow, and he believed that in the long run his best chance to gain the boy-king's friendship was through the mother. Furthermore, Marie had a staggering private fortune, and Richelieu always liked to be where money was.

So into exile he went, to another test of patience. For seven years he had to restrain that burning desire to rule. He wrote letters, and more letters, to everybody who could be of use to him. He kept himself informed as to what was happening everywhere. And he devoted himself to the middle-aged, bitter Queen. He talked with her, read to her, and even learned to play music so as to entertain her. She was so grateful to him for his advice and loyalty that she gave him and his family huge sums of money.

THE RETURN

Richelieu's career at this point shows just how the mind of a dictator works.

A number of nobles on the Queen's side—the old Concini group—were impatient to get back into power, so that they could once more dip their hands in the royal treasury. They persuaded the brooding Queen to lead an armed revolt against Luynes's government. Richelieu saw that such a revolt could not possibly succeed. But to the Queen he said, in effect, "Yes, it seems like a good idea. Go ahead." The rebellion broke out suddenly, and some towns and provinces were seized before Louis's army could take the field.

Marie's troops were scattered, however, and her generals advised her to avoid a big battle. Their hope was to attack and pillage the helpless border provinces until the King grew tired of it and gave them what they wanted in order to have peace. But to everybody's surprise, Richelieu disagreed and urged a quick, decisive war. As usual, his eloquence had its way with the Queen, and her army awaited the King's soldiers.

Richelieu knew that the Queen's troops were certain to be defeated. But the last thing he wanted was a long struggle, which would have wrecked his chances of obtaining the young King's friendship. Apparently without feeling any shame over his treachery, he had secretly written to Louis and Luynes.

Here, he told them, was their chance to break the power of the rebel lords. And at the same time, if they were generous, they could end the unnatural breach between mother and son. Louis approved, and Richelieu undertook to see that the Queen's weak troops stood their ground. Stood their ground, that is, for a few minutes; they fled almost at the first musket volley.

Richelieu's trick succeeded just as he had planned. Hardly was the battle over when Marie and Louis were reconciled. Although Marie probably knew what her favorite had done, she was grateful, in view of the outcome. As a reward, she urged Louis to nominate Richelieu for cardinal of the Church.

To make things easier for Richelieu, about this time his enemy Luynes died of a fever. Louis consented to send the nomination to Rome. And the Pope quickly confirmed it, in the mistaken hope that once Richelieu was a cardinal, he would be more friendly to the policies of the Church.

Then the King invited the new cardinal to sit once again as a member of the council. Like everyone else in the council meetings, Louis was tremendously impressed by Richelieu's ability, and after three months the King appointed him prime minister of France.

THE ENEMIES OF RICHELIEU

But Richelieu was by no means a popular man. Few politicians have succeeded in the face of such formidable enemies as he had.

The Church feared him, and strict Catholics disapproved of his leniency toward the Protestants. Curiously, the Protestants hated him too, because although he permitted them to practice their religion, he refused to let them set up the governments they wanted in their cities.

Spain, Austria, and England were all opposed to this man who had openly declared his intention to make France greater than all other countries. They tried many plots to discredit him. In some of these plots, as you will remember from reading *The Three Musketeers,* Louis's beautiful Spanish Queen, Anne of Austria, took part, for she detested the cardinal. And a number of nobles joined in the attacks on him under the leadership of the king's own brother, Gaston of Orléans.

Even the Dowager Queen Marie, his former patroness, soon became Richelieu's enemy. She had hoped that when he was prime minister, he would do whatever she wanted. When she found that he would not allow her to interfere with his plans, she became furious, and tried to persuade the King to get rid of him. But while the King often resented Richelieu, as inferior men always resent genius, nevertheless he feared and respected and needed him too much to risk losing him.

Of course Richelieu had some supporters, too. Some of the French clergy were working quietly for him under the leadership of Father Joseph. More important still, the business men of France, the tradesmen and merchants and lawyers, were on his side, for they hoped that he would help them shake off their feudal tax burdens. It was only by the support of the middle class that he was able to build up the great army and secret service that were to make him master of France.

THE CARDINAL STRIKES

Hardly had Richelieu become prime minister, when he struck at his enemies, all together. First he sent an army against the rebellious Protestants and defeated them quickly. And he began a small war against Austria by seizing a certain important mountain pass in the Alps. He realized that Austria and Spain were no longer the mighty countries that most people thought them, and this attack of his was like snapping his fingers in the Emperor's face.

At the same time he forbade certain members of the royal family to draw money from the King's treasury. Naturally, there was a hurricane of aristocratic indignation. Queen Anne, Queen Marie, Gaston of Orléans, and their followers determined to get rid of this man who dared oppose them. The Queens sent secret agents to obtain the aid of Spain, and they also conspired with the English ambassador, the Duke of Buckingham.

But the Cardinal's spies were everywhere, and they knew what was going on. Richelieu obtained evidence that the King's own family was in league with enemy countries, and he pretended that the plot was directed against Louis himself. The King was enraged, and when he was in a rage he was not a weak man. He thundered against the culprits, and the conspiracy fell apart. Some nobles were arrested and executed; Buckingham fled to England; and Queen Anne lost her influence over her husband. As a result of all this, Richelieu was able to obtain from the King complete authority over the army, the navy, and the treasury. He had risked everything on this stroke, and had won.

RICHELIEU ATTACKS THE FEUDAL SYSTEM

The Cardinal was now practically the dictator of France. But he and the King were alarmed over the question of money. The royal treasury was terribly in debt, and more money had to be found without delay.

Richelieu's plan was to force the peasants and business men of France to pay more of their taxes to the Crown, and less to the feudal lords. Of course, the nobles were sure to object, but at the

moment they were all cowed by the exposure of the great conspiracy. Furthermore, the Cardinal was able to pacify nobles
whom he liked by giving them pensions and gifts, which partly
made up for their lost taxes. He was determined to send out his
own tax collectors, and build up a great centralized system, so
that he could run the money matters of the entire country from
his palace in Paris.

Of course, this meant that some very important new laws had
to be passed. Richelieu was too wise merely to issue these really
revolutionary laws by royal decree. It was necessary to make the
peasants, artisans, and tradesmen understand and approve the
new system. Otherwise they might have stubbornly clung to
their old ways and refused to pay their taxes to the King's men.

In order to persuade the people to support him, Richelieu had to
call some kind of assembly together, which would appear to
represent popular feeling, and which would approve his new
laws. He did not dare summon the traditional body, the States
General, for it was certain to be controlled by his enemies among
the nobility and the clergy. The Cardinal wanted a hand-picked
assembly—just as Mussolini and Hitler today have parliaments
made up entirely of their proven supporters. The purpose of
such imitation parliaments is to make people believe that they
have something to say about how they are governed. Actually,
of course, the men who sit in these assemblies are not the people's
representatives, but the dictator's.

Richelieu called his assembly a "Council of Notables," and he
selected the members largely from among lawyers, merchants,
and the minor nobility. These men were all enthusiastic about
Richelieu's plans, because they believed that the new laws would
mean lower taxes and higher profits for them.

Time would show that they were mistaken. For the Cardinal was himself an aristocrat, and in his secret thoughts cared little about trade and commerce, except as they helped to make France and Richelieu mighty. At first, however, he pretended that he was the benefactor of business. He agreed to end many of the feudal "nuisance-laws" that annoyed the merchants. He agreed further to protect the peaceful classes against the feudal troops, and to give royal grants, or subsidies, to certain enterprises. Naturally, the Council of Notables was grateful, and agreed in its turn to approve the new laws, so that almost before anyone realized what was happening, the common people of France were paying most of their taxes to Richelieu's agents.

The new laws also allowed Richelieu to build up a great standing army under the royal command—something new in those days—and to construct France's first royal navy. The immense spy system which he had organized was also a novelty. But then, Richelieu had a bold, original mind. In fact, he may be called the first great modern dictator, for he established the methods which all "successful" dictators since his day have followed.

"THE DAY OF DUPES"

After the defeat of the first great conspiracy against Richelieu, the Duke of Buckingham and the English nobility determined to make another effort to crush him. So they urged the French city of La Rochelle, which was a Protestant stronghold, to revolt again, and sent ships and men to assist in the struggle. A short, bitter war followed, in which the Cardinal commanded the King's army in person, and out-generaled Buckingham at every point. After a ruthless siege, La Rochelle fell to the royal troops.

Everybody expected Richelieu to close all Protestant churches in revenge. But he was too shrewd to try anything of the kind. He was determined to have no more religious strife. So long as the Protestants obeyed the King's laws, he did not try to force them to obey Rome's.

While he was at the battle front, another plot against him was hatched in Paris, with the King's mother as the leader. The plotters were wiser this time. They would give Richelieu no opportunity to pretend that their attack on him was an attack on the Crown. Instead, Marie played on the King's pride. Was he, Louis XIII, willing to let this upstart Richelieu make him a mere puppet-king, the laughing-stock of European royalty? Was the Crown of France to become only a symbol?

The King had felt and resented the Cardinal's growing power. As day after day the vengeful Queen pleaded openly for the dismissal of the arrogant minister, Louis began to incline more and more to his mother's views. He would prove who was ruler of France!

Richelieu returned to court to find a scowl on the King's face. The rumor spread that he had asked for a private audience, and had been refused. Everyone was sure that he was doomed. Paris seethed with excitement. Large numbers of the feudal nobility, thinking to be on the winning side, hastened to pledge their loyalty to Marie and Gaston of Orleans. The Cardinal's supporters were panicky. It was common gossip that the Queen-Mother was about to make a final plea to her son, and that Richelieu would be thrust from power or destroyed.

The awaited day came—and the aristocrats of France found that they had been duped again. Richelieu was still minister. The King had granted him an audience, and publicly approved his actions. Like frightened sheep, the great nobles flocked again to make their peace with the incredible man who had once more converted disaster into triumph.

Never did Richelieu's genius reveal itself more clearly than in his dramatic success on the so-called "Day of Dupes." Everybody had been expecting some desperate plot from him. Instead, he faced his chief enemy boldly and frankly. His spies told him that Marie was to see the King for the final conference at such-and-such a time, in a certain room of a certain palace. The doors were to be locked against intruders. But there was a servants' entrance to the room, and Richelieu took pains to see that that entrance remained unlocked. At the very moment when Marie was denouncing him, he flung open the servants' door. Standing there in his red cardinal's robes, with a faint smile on his face, he said quietly, "I will wager that your Majesties are talking about me."

Marie was startled, furious. She cried out her accusations to Richelieu's face. But he was a great actor, as well as a great statesman. With tears in his eyes, he knelt before the King. Whatever he had done, he said in a hushed voice, had been for the glory of France and the Crown. At all points he had been loyal to the dynasty. His power was the King's. And France and the throne were stronger than ever before.

It was true, and the King knew it. Richelieu might love authority, but he respected the principle of monarchy. And in his heart Louis was aware that he could not govern alone. Without Richelieu, the machinery of the state would break down, the dukes would reclaim their old rights, civil wars would flare up again. He demanded time to consider, but only one decision was possible. Richelieu remained in office.

And remained, furthermore, even stronger than before. The King no longer opposed him on any point. Those courtiers who had supported Marie were exiled from France in droves. Finally Richelieu demanded that Louis banish Marie herself. There was no talk now about mother and son. Louis was torn, but he obeyed, and Marie was forced to go to Flanders. There she died in poverty—a woman not wise enough to know when she had met her master.

THE SOLDIER-CARDINAL

While Richelieu was crushing his enemies, the Empire of the Habsburgs was being exhausted by the Thirty Years' War between Catholics and Protestants in Germany. Sometimes this long and terrible conflict seemed to favor one side, sometimes the other. Richelieu, although a cardinal of the Catholic Church, determined to help the Protestants—not because he wanted to spread the Protestant religion, but because he wanted to see Austria still further weakened for the benefit of France and Richelieu.

He did not, however, wish to involve France in war just yet. His idea was to help the Protestants with money. The Protestant Swedish King, the famous Gustavus Adolphus, was then invading Germany to attack the imperial forces. He was badly in need of funds with which to pay his armies; so Richelieu sent him several tubs of gold.

Gustavus Adolphus won a series of remarkable victories, and for a while it looked as if he would smash the Empire completely. In fact, Richelieu began to feel uneasy, for he had no desire to see the Catholic Church destroyed in Austria. However, Gustavus was killed in battle, and the tide began to turn again in favor of the Habsburgs.

The Cardinal decided that the time had come for France to march. Austria, he suspected, was in no position to offer much resistance. But this was an error. The Austrians were good fighters, and they were furious at France, while the French Catholics did not really want the war. Several battles were won by the imperial armies, and at one time they actually invaded France.

To make matters more serious for Richelieu, the cost of the war was very high. He had to call on business men and nobles alike to pay larger taxes, and still larger. They were angry, but they were too much afraid of him to disobey. In time his troops managed to drive the Austrians out.

The war moved on from victory to defeat, and from defeat to victory, all equally useless, until everybody in France was complaining. As the complaints became louder, the Cardinal's measures became harsher. Like any modern dictator, he would allow no news to be printed unless he approved it. He would permit no parliament to assemble. His spies sought out every man who dared speak against him, and such poor devils were sent to prison by the thousands.

Although taxes were twice as high as they had been in "the good old days of Henri IV," the government's expenses were higher yet. The royal treasury owed six times as much money to bankers and money lenders as it had before Richelieu became dictator. Every peasant had to pay a special tax, called a head-tax, just for being alive.

This tax was particularly hateful. Some peasants were so poor that they could not scrape together the few pennies needed, and in such cases their neighbors were forced to put up the money for them. In Normandy the peasants were so angry that they tried to rebel. The Cardinal hired foreign troops to crush this revolt, because he did not think that French troops would be cruel enough. Hundreds of poor farmers were tortured, and thousands killed, and every Norman business man who had any money had to give most of it to the state "as punishment."

THE HATRED OF FRANCE

Richelieu cared nothing for human life or suffering. In this he was like most dictators. Years later Napoleon said, "He who feels pity is lost," and this un-Christian sentiment is the key of the dictator's mind.

From year to year the Cardinal's tyrannies became harder and harder to bear. Under the old system, even though the peasantry and artisans were oppressed, the Three Estates, at least, had had certain rights and liberties. Now no one had any rights, and liberty was dead. Even the King no longer questioned his all-powerful minister, who held in his hands every instrument of power—army, navy, tax collectors, spies, foreign envoys. When some courtiers dared attempt another conspiracy against him, Richelieu crushed it with terrifying ease; he executed the King's favorite, exiled the King's brother, made a wealthy duke give up his vast estates for a pardon. Not even the greatest noble in the land was sure of his life if he said "No" when Richelieu wished him to say "Yes."

France, from the humblest peasant to the richest aristocrat, hated him. Everywhere he went he had to be surrounded by a vast bodyguard to prevent his assassination. Only those who owed their positions to him could be trusted—and then only while he paid them.

But he did not care. Grimly he persisted in his war, and sent an army to invade Spain. Finally the Habsburgs sued for peace, and gave up certain territories. France at last was master in the affairs of Europe.

No one can say what Richelieu's next move would have been, for at this point, in 1642, he died quietly in his bed. For some time his health had been failing, owing to overwork. The good news from Spain came to him during his illness, but he still remembered his duty to the King, and he sent him a last message, saying: "Sire, your arms have triumphed and your enemies have perished!" Then he summoned a priest to administer the final rites of the Church.

Even dying, he was still the same Richelieu, the same masterful man. The priest asked him, "Do you pardon your enemies?" The old fire flashed for an instant in the Cardinal's eyes. "Enemies? I have none—except those of the state!"

With his death, France breathed a sigh of relief. Everybody began to sing a new popular song, which went, "Now he is dead and put away." The King himself announced that the laws would be relaxed, and he opened the prisons and revoked orders of banishment. Once more the great nobles swaggered about the court, quarreling and plotting, and once more France began to sway dangerously toward civil war.

AFTERWARD

Yet in the difficult times that followed, the government that Richelieu had built endured. He made the French throne absolute, and absolute it remained until the year 1789. No doubt you have read romances and seen motion pictures of the glamorous days of Louis XIV, Louis XV, and Louis XVI. Certainly, life glittered then. The kings and nobles enjoyed fabulous riches and pleasures. Some merchants and bankers grew rich. But it was different with the people—the ordinary people—people like most of us today.

From year to year, under the dictatorship of the Bourbon kings, the people grew poorer, more oppressed. It is hard for us, living today in wealthy, democratic America, to imagine the misery of millions of French peasants in the 1700's. A dozen times they revolted against the tax collectors, until they were cowed by the bullets of the King's musketeers. Thousands of peasants left their little patches of land and became beggars. Women carrying a loaf of bread were murdered by poor men insane with hunger. Rags were usual clothing. Men lived like animals. The peasant who had a few pennies or a little food dared not let anyone know it, lest he be robbed, or sent to prison as a suspicious character.

Of course, no nation can hold together long under such conditions. The government ran more and more into debt. Taxes grew higher. French nobles and merchants began to go bankrupt. And at last, in utter desperation, business men, artisans, peasants, and some aristocrats joined in a great revolution, and ended the old despotism with fire and bloodshed.

Certainly, this is not what Richelieu planned and worked for. When he began, he expected to make France a great and prosperous nation. But as the chapters which follow show, what a dictator hopes for and what he actually accomplishes are two very different things.

A nation under the whip of a despot may sometimes win wars for a while, but the taste of victory in time becomes stale in the mouths of the people. Sooner or later they see through the empty talk about "glory" and "power." They begin to dream of having enough to eat; of owning a new dress, or suit of clothes; of freedom to dance and sing and talk and read as they choose; of peace of mind and the knowledge that their sweethearts, husbands, wives, and children are safe at home. And then they discover what so many other peoples have discovered before them—that they can have these wonderful gifts of life only if they have a voice in the making of their country's laws—the voice which we call democracy.

Cromwell

Cromwell Leads a Revolution

WHEN haughty, handsome Charles I, ruler of England and Scotland, came to the throne in 1625, he thought he knew how to be a successful king. It was very easy. You had only to go to war, and win, and take the wealth of some other country. His idea was to attack Spain, which had a great deal of gold, but not much of a navy.

But in order to make war, you had to have money. What a nuisance! The royal treasury was empty. There would have to be some new taxes.

According to the great English tradition, the King could not ask the people to pay new taxes and give him money until he had received the consent of Parliament. So Charles summoned Parliament and rather impatiently told it what he wanted.

Then as now, the English Parliament consisted of two Houses, "The Lords" and "The Commons." The Lords are members by right of their aristocratic birth; the Commons are elected by the people. The Lords in Charles's Parliament did not want to pay more taxes themselves. But they were willing to let the King tax the business men. The House of Commons, however, was full of business men, and they objected.

One of the reasons why Parliament refused to do anything

about new taxes was that it did not trust the King's chief minister and favorite, the elegant Duke of Buckingham—the same who fought against Richelieu. Buckingham sucked up money like a sponge, and always needed more, but the only people who ever got any benefit from all the money he collected were his friends and the friends of the King. These lucky courtiers built beautiful palaces, and had wonderful clothes and jewels, while most of the people in England did not have enough to eat. So the members of the Commons said to each other, "Why give our money to Buckingham, or to a king who does just what Buckingham wants him to do?"

KING AGAINST PARLIAMENT

When Charles found that his first Parliament would not give him money, he sent the members home, and called for new elections. But this did not help him. The second Parliament was even more stubborn than the first. The royal favorite Buckingham was again sharply criticized for his spendthrift ways and for his failure in the war against Richelieu.

Charles, raging, got rid of this Parliament, too. For a while he managed to borrow money here and there. But soon he was more desperate than ever. A third time he summoned Parliament, and grimly warned it not to criticize, but to supply him with money at once. Again he was refused. The House of Commons proclaimed that the Duke of Buckingham was the cause of the nation's troubles, and said they would not do anything about new taxes while he was in office.

Soon afterward, the Duke of Buckingham was murdered. Angry past endurance, the King blamed the Commons for the murder. To teach them a lesson, he decided on a bold step—to raise taxes without the consent of Parliament. All at once he decreed that merchants had to pay a duty called "tonnage and poundage" on all goods which they brought into the country from abroad.

At this there was a great outcry in Parliament. For if Charles succeeded in enforcing this tax, then Parliament's chief powers were gone, together with rights for which the common people of England had been fighting for centuries. Some merchants preferred to go to prison rather than pay the new tax. All England was in an uproar. No one knew what would happen next.

"THE MEMBER FOR HUNTINGDON"

If you had been alive in those stirring times, and had been living in London, you might well have paid a visit to the House of Commons. For everybody was excited about the great quarrel between the King and Parliament, and wanted to hear the speeches and know what was going on. You would have sat in the gallery from which the public was permitted to look on, and tried to find where such famous leaders of the Commons as John Hampden and John Pym were sitting.

Now if the day of your visit happened to be February 11, 1629, you would have seen a historic event. But you would not have realized at the time that anything remarkable was happening. It began when a young man rose to his feet in the rear of the great hall, and said, "Mr. Speaker!" The Speaker, or chief officer of the House of Commons, looked down from his raised platform, and answered, "The honorable member for Huntingdon"— which meant that the member had permission to speak.

The young man was tall and strong, and wore a plain woolen suit. His face was rather homely; he had a large nose, and there was a big wart on his forehead, and another on his chin. But his eyes were keen and bright, and he held himself erect, in a dignified way. And although he had a harsh voice and was not a very good speaker, nevertheless he put a great deal of sincerity and feeling into his words. A certain bishop, he said, was trying to bring the Catholic religion back to Protestant England. Would Parliament permit it?

Possibly you might have turned, and asked your neighbor if he knew the name of that young man who was speaking. If your neighbor happened to be a nobleman or fashionable gentleman, he would probably have wrinkled his nose in disgust and, dusting a particle of snuff from his embroidered coat with a lace handkerchief, answered, "What matter the names of these preaching Puritan hypocrites? They are all alike. How I would like to try a whip on them!"

But if a knowing tradesman of London heard your question, he might well have said to you, with an approving nod, "That is Master Oliver Cromwell, a cousin to our good Master Hampden. He owns farm and grazing lands in Cambridgeshire, and does a thriving trade in wool. An excellent man of the Lord is Master Cromwell, for they do say he is wonderfully apt at leading prayer or hymn, or quoting Holy Writ."

"Master Oliver Cromwell." Many times afterward you would hear that name. And in the years to come, sitting among your children and grandchildren, you would proudly relate how you were present in the House of Commons when "my Lord General Cromwell, Protector of England," made his first speech in Parliament.

THE PURITANS

Cromwell was, of course, on the side of the business men against the King. But as you would have learned from his speech, this trouble over taxes was only one of the great quarrels that was tearing England apart. Even more important was the religious struggle.

A century earlier, King Henry VIII had taken away the property of the Roman Catholic Church in England, and set up an English, or Anglican, Church, with himself as its head. But presently many Englishmen began to disapprove of the new religion, because it was still too much like Roman Catholicism for their taste. They wanted to "purify" the English Church, as they put it. By Cromwell's time, these "Puritans" had become very numerous, and had set up their own churches, and were refusing to attend the Church of England. Some of them had gone to America to find religious freedom.

For the most part, the Puritans were sincere men who read the Bible constantly and regarded it as law, and who were willing to give their lives for the right to worship as they chose. But many of them went around with long faces, and thought that to have fun and to laugh often was to be disrespectful to the Lord. They quoted the Bible and prayed on the least excuse. Some of them had an affected way of speaking through their noses, because they thought it sounded "religious." One can understand why people who did not share their views often regarded them as hypocrites, or fanatics.

When Oliver Cromwell was a boy, attending a private school, he heard a great deal about religion. It affected him strangely, for he grew very melancholy, and often thought he was sick and going to die when there was nothing really wrong with him. Later on, he went to the great University of Cambridge. There he turned into a more normal youth, and even went out with girls and gambled, which shocked the Puritans, who were strong in Cambridge. Soon, however, he became sorry about these "mistakes," and paid back the money he had won at dice. From this point on he was more and more religious. By the time he reached manhood, he belonged to a group of Puritans called "Independents," who believed that everybody had the right to worship God according to his own private conscience, without having to obey the bishops of the King's Church, or to pay them money.

CHARLES TRIES TO BE A DICTATOR

Let us get back now to Parliament and "tonnage and poundage." For some time the House of Commons was terribly excited. What was to be done? Many of the members, Cromwell among them, wanted to protest against the King's action in strong language. But the King had his supporters, too. The debates grew fierce. Cromwell, it is said, swore that if the House did not protest, he would go to America to seek freedom. But finally he and his friends had their way. Parliament said the King had exceeded his rights, and they told the people of England not to pay the new tax.

Charles was furious. Was he, the King, to permit rebellion by a handful of merchants and lawyers and stiff-necked Puritans? He gave orders that Parliament be closed. Moreover, he threw nine leaders of the Commons into prison. He would show England what sort of king he was! Did not his cousin Louis XIII of

France, or, at any rate, his minister Richelieu, rule without a parliament? Well, then, Charles Stuart would likewise rule by royal decree! That, he said, was his "divine right."

And for eleven years, despite the protests of the people, rule by decree he did. But Charles was no Richelieu; he was not cunning, or farsighted, or original, or careful. Most of the important nobles supported him, but each new tax made life harder to bear for the poor of England, and angered the business men. Year by year, his hold on the loyalty of his people grew weaker. And the King was not clever enough to build up a well-paid spy system and a large standing army to support him, as Richelieu had done.

The greatest mistake a king or a statesman can make is not to realize that times change, and laws and governments must change with them if trouble is to be avoided. The English people would never again be quiet under tyranny. Charles did not see this. Nor did he understand how ordinary men and women thought and felt about life. He wanted to be just, but he did not know how important a few pennies a day can be to poor people, and how necessary it is for them to get their money's worth when they buy something.

SOAP AND EARS

His attempt to raise money by going into the soap business shows how little he understood his subjects. He said to one or two soap manufacturers, in effect, "Look here, I will make a law that will forbid the English people to buy soap from anybody but you. We will drive the other soap manufacturers out of business. This will mean a great profit for you. And in return, you must give me a big share of your profit."

This kind of arrangement was called a monopoly. Nowadays, of course, we try to prevent business men and politicians from taking advantage of an entire nation in that way; but in Charles's time it was customary for kings to create monopolies. There probably would have been no great trouble about the soap had it not been that the King's manufacturers became greedier and greedier. First they raised the price of soap. Then they replaced the good soap with cheap soap, until finally it was not soap at all, but some substance that blistered the hands without cleansing them.

The English are a cleanly people, and had to have soap, but they deeply resented paying good money for blistered skins. There were "soap riots" all over England. But Charles liked the way the money was coming in from the monopoly. For a long while he refused to make the manufacturers improve the quality of the soap; and this one mistake cost him the good will of hundreds of thousands of his subjects.

Furthermore, now that Charles was dictator of England, he tried to force the Puritans to join the Church of England. Some of the Puritan leaders he punished by the cutting off of their ears. These cruelties made thousands of Englishmen grit their teeth and dream of revenge.

You cannot cork up a people's justifiable indignation forever. In time it explodes. Charles's few soldiers kept London quiet. But up in Scotland, the Puritans suddenly revolted against some of Charles's bishops. He sent troops to crush the rebels; but the men were ill-paid and mistreated by their officers, so they mutinied.

Charles saw that he had to raise a loyal army, and be quick about it. But, as usual, he had no money. He asked the bankers of

London to lend him a large sum. They answered that they would do so only if Parliament approved. Then he asked some of the great nobles of England. They too advised him to summon Parliament. At last, to his intense humiliation, Charles had to give in.

Charles hoped to get his money and then to send Parliament away at once. But the members, with Cromwell among them again, knew this. They made Charles sign a law which prevented him from dissolving Parliament except by its own consent. And even then he was not permitted to use the money he received for war against the Scots. On the contrary, he had to make peace with them, pardon them, and withdraw his bishops. Furthermore, Charles had to consent to the imprisonment and execution of Lord Strafford, his chief adviser, who was hated by the people.

THE FIGHT BEGINS

The members of Parliament became afraid that if they annoyed the King any more, he would declare them to be in a state of rebellion, and send troops against them. So they demanded that he grant them the right to raise troops.

This right was the real heart of the King's power, and he indignantly refused to give it up. Instead he decided on a bold move—to arrest his most dangerous enemies in the Commons on the ground of treason against their King. First, he told Parliament to yield them up. Parliament refused. Charles grew pale with anger, and, summoning several hundred soldiers, rode to the House of Commons, to make the arrests himself. The men whom he wanted, however, had hidden themselves in London, and the King feared that if he pursued them, the city would riot against him.

Now he had gone too far for anything but open war. If he was to make Parliament and the Puritans obey him, he had to raise a large army, and at once. Many of the nobility and landed gentry all over England and Scotland would rally to their King. Charles left his palace in London and rode north, calling for volunteers, and for donations of gold and silver.

In that thrilling year, 1642, Oliver Cromwell was forty-three years old. His great rise to fame, as you see, came rather late—quite unlike Richelieu's. During the time that the King ruled without Parliament Cromwell had been running his farms, growing crops, trading in wool—and studying.

Although a serious man, much given to prayer and religious discussion, Cromwell was far from being meek or humble. When his ideas of what was right and just were offended, his temper could be fierce. Once he was a member of a Parliamentary Committee, which was trying to decide an important law case. A nobleman had bought some land and found that there were some poor farmers living on it. He told the farmers to get out—which was like telling them to starve. They answered that while they paid their rent, he had no right to put them off the land. When the case came before Parliament, Cromwell took the side of the peasants, and stormed against the nobleman until the Committee had to caution him for his violence.

But as yet nobody thought of him as an outstanding leader. While the King was raising his army, Cromwell sat in the House listening to other men's speeches, with a frown on his face. Speeches! The time for speeches had gone by!

Some members of Parliament were nervous about actually declaring war on their King. Half-heartedly they sent a committee to try to make some kind of peace with Charles. Cromwell's frown became deeper. Months were passing, the King's troops were being trained—and all Parliament did was talk! Well, let others hang back! He would take his stand frankly as a rebel, fight for his religion, and his political rights as an Englishman. Impatiently, he asked permission to raise two companies of volunteers in Cambridge, and received it.

Now he was Captain Cromwell, drilling several hundred mounted men. Another month, and he boldly seized the King's arsenal at Cambridge, where there were swords, armor, and muskets. Then he led his men into the University, and removed all the valuable gold and silver objects which it owned, so as to prevent them from being given to the King. Soon his troops were searching out royalists everywhere in the shire, and making sure that they did not help the King's cause. Cromwell was happy, for he loved action, and was a natural commander of men.

He even brought his eldest son, Oliver, whom he dearly loved, into the army. "Thou too, boy Oliver," he said, "thou art fit to swing a sword. If ever was a battle worth fighting, and to be called God's battle, it is this. Thou too wilt come." When later he heard that young Oliver was killed in battle, he could not speak. He shut himself up in a room and sat for hours, with his face buried in his hands, praying; for this was the greatest grief of his life.

THE IRONSIDES

At last Parliament assembled an army, fourteen thousand in all, under the command of the Earl of Essex, one of the few nobles on the rebel side. Then came the first serious battle of the war. It was won by the royalists. The rebel infantry fought bravely enough, but the King's cavalry, commanded by his dashing nephew, Prince Rupert, completely routed the cavalry of Parliament. However, a few troops among the rebel horsemen put up a fight; and among these were the companies of Captain Oliver Cromwell.

This battle taught Cromwell a great lesson. The King's cavalry was composed largely of young gentlemen, "cavaliers," who had been taught from childhood to handle weapons, and to be physically brave and reckless, and who considered it a disgrace to run from a fight. Against men like these, the ordinary workmen and shop apprentices of the towns could not be expected to stand their ground, for they lacked the fighting spirit. But then, Cromwell asked himself, were there no men on the rebel side who could beat these cavaliers at their own game—be just as brave and reckless, and better disciplined? If there were none, then the cause of Parliament was lost. But there were! He would raise a regiment of sincere Puritans—"men who had the fear of God before them," men who would go into battle singing hymns, and who were as willing to die for their religion as the cavaliers for their honor.

He spent several months seeking out and recruiting such men among the Roundheads, as the rebels, with their short haircuts, were called. Soon he became a colonel, and commanded a whole regiment of cavalry, whose wonderful courage and daring later earned them the name of the Ironsides. Within a year he had helped to win several important battles, and had shown so much bravery and skill that he was commissioned Lieutenant-General.

You may ask, how is it that this gentleman-farmer, who had never before been to war, and had no military training, was almost from the beginning such a remarkable soldier? Most historians believe that Cromwell had carefully studied the wars of the Swedish King Gustavus Adolphus in Germany. What he learned about military strategy from these brilliant campaigns, together with his natural talents, made him the great general that he was.

CROMWELL WINS FOR PARLIAMENT

But although at bloody Marston Moor Cromwell's men out-charged Prince Rupert's fierce cavalry and won the day, else-where the tide of battle was going against the Roundhead armies. The noble earls, Essex and Manchester, who were the chief generals of Parliament, were not good military leaders. Cromwell knew his own abilities now, and he felt that the rebel army would win if he were in command. Essex and Manchester had to be removed.

To Parliament, of which he was still a member, Cromwell sent a message pointing out the mistakes of the Earl of Manchester. Manchester replied angrily. A great quarrel took place in Parliament between the supporters of both men. Then somebody had an idea. Let all members of Parliament "deny themselves" military rank. Make it a law that no member of Parliament could also be an army officer. This would be fair all around, since it would affect not only Cromwell, but also Manchester and Essex, who were members of the House of Lords.

This "Self-Denying Ordinance" was quickly agreed on by everybody, including Cromwell. Manchester and Essex at once gave up their army commands, and Cromwell said that he would do so. A general named Sir Thomas Fairfax was appointed as the new commander-in-chief.

But now it appeared that there was nothing to prevent a member of Parliament who had given up his army command from

being reappointed! Sir Thomas at once made Cromwell Lieutenant-General again. In this way Cromwell got rid of his opponents, and became the real leader of the rebel armies.

The first thing he did—and this shows his wisdom—was to
make sure that no matter where his troops marched, plans were
made to feed them properly. He knew that no man can be a good
soldier unless he has enough to eat; as Napoleon later said, "An
army marches on its stomach." Under Manchester, the rebel
troops had always been complaining about the lack of supplies
and had lost courage and hope, but Cromwell's "New Model"
army, as he called it, had plenty of fighting spirit.

Steadily he and Fairfax drove back the royalist forces. Finally
Charles could fight no more. In 1647 he surrendered, and was put
under guard in a palace. But he was still King. No one as yet
talked of executing him, and people thought that he would soon
make peace with Parliament and go back to his throne, a wiser
man.

CROMWELL QUARRELS WITH PARLIAMENT

Most of the members of Parliament were very eager to have
the King back, if he would give them control of taxes and troops.
Already riotous gangs were roaming the streets of London,
threatening Parliament and demanding all kinds of outrageous
laws. The King's name was needed to restore order.

Although Cromwell did not think that any good could come
of putting Charles back on the throne, he did not openly oppose
Parliament on this point. But there was one serious question on
which he violently disagreed—the question of religion.

The majority of Parliament was in favor of making the Presbyterian religion the new official religion of England instead of

the Anglican Church. This did not suit Cromwell in the least. He had nothing against the Presbyterian religion, but as a stanch Independent he wanted to get rid of an "established" Church in England once and for all—no matter what its religion was.

The Presbyterian majority in Parliament was a little afraid of Cromwell, because they knew that the army would back him up. So they gave orders that the army be disbanded. They had another strong reason, besides. The soldiers had fought without pay for a long while, and now they were demanding money. And there was no money in the treasury. The politicians in Parliament hoped that if they sent the men home with a vague promise about paying "in the future," the question of payment would be gradually forgotten.

When Cromwell heard this, he was terribly disheartened. He felt that after all the army and he had done for Parliament, they were being ungratefully pushed aside. A mood of black despair seized him. He thought of leaving England and going to fight for the Protestants in Germany.

But soon his courage revived. He struggled between his loyalty to Parliament and what he believed was right. Then he made up his mind. Instead of disbanding his troops, he gave them orders to march on London.

To Parliament he said that he was coming to protect it against the London mobs. But the politicians were even more afraid of the army than of the mobs. After bitter arguments, they persuaded Cromwell to keep his men outside the city, and in return they reluctantly agreed to let him and the army make the terms of peace with the King.

CHARLES MEETS HIS DOOM

There was no real hope that Charles and Cromwell would ever agree. The King saw that the country was growing restless under Parliament's rule. He knew that up in Scotland the Presbyterians were angry over Parliament's failure to set up a Presbyterian Church of England, and were ready to change over to his side. His hopes soared again. One night he managed to escape from his guard, and desperately rode north to rally the Scots to his standard.

When Cromwell heard the news, he was not at all upset. One can imagine that he smiled grimly as he buckled on his sword, and called his officers around him. The question of who was to rule England had to be settled once and for all; and how settle it, except by war?

So the Second Civil War began. Again Cromwell scored victory after victory, until finally Charles's Scottish troops, who had never really cared much for the King, treacherously agreed to "sell him" to the English as a prisoner.

But no sooner had the war ended than the same old quarrel broke out between Parliament and Cromwell over the question of a settlement with Charles. This time Cromwell was in no mood for half-way measures. "Are we," he asked bitterly, "to have a little bit of paper for all our fighting?" He sent part of his army into London, and a number of troops, headed by a certain Colonel Pride, sternly marched to the House of Commons. There the colonel stood at the door, with a list of the hundreds of members in his hand, and he refused to allow any members to take their places in the House except about sixty who were friendly to Cromwell. These became known in history as the "Rump Parliament."

The first thing the Rump did was to try the King on the ground of treason and condemn him to death by the headsman's ax. For this Cromwell has been bitterly reproached. Many writers of history say that it was cruel and unnecessary. Cruel perhaps it was, although it does not hurt a king to die any more than a common man. But was it unnecessary? To Cromwell, the first great need was to restore peace to England, to set up a strong government with freedom of worship, and prevent a further outbreak of civil war. While Charles lived, many hotheaded royalists would be wanting to fight for him again, and thousands of men might be killed in useless battles. Was it not better, Cromwell reasoned, that the King should die?

Probably Cromwell was wrong in thinking this. Things might well have been better for the common people of England and everybody else if Charles had lived, and had been made to obey a lawful Parliament. But Cromwell could not guess the future, and he acted in all sincerity for what he thought was the good of the country.

At any rate, Charles died with dignity, like the proud gentleman he was, and the Rump Parliament set to work to rule what was no longer called the "Kingdom of England," but the "Commonwealth, or Free State."

THE RUMP OPPOSES CROMWELL

For the next few years Cromwell had a great amount of fighting to do. First he had to deal with a new English political party who called themselves the Levellers, and who wanted to reform the new government, and to make sure that everybody in England was equal in rank and wealth with everybody else. In fact, they had ideas which we today would call "socialistic," and which seemed very strange indeed in those days, although they are more familiar now. Many of the soldiers became Levellers, and some of them mutinied when Parliament refused to grant their demands.

When Cromwell had put down this mutiny, he had to defeat rebel armies in Ireland and Scotland. And then a great naval war broke out with Holland. In those days Dutch ships carried most of the goods between the different ports in western Europe, and Dutch shipowners and Dutch merchants made much more money than the shipowners and merchants of other countries. To prevent other nations from trying to share in their profits, Holland had built the strongest navy in Europe.

For some time English and Dutch merchants had been quarreling, and there was much hard feeling. Cromwell persuaded Parliament to postpone the war until England could build as many ships as the Dutch had. Finally the enlarged navy sailed out under the famous Admiral Blake and, in a series of great sea victories, broke Holland's might.

While Blake was "beating the Dutch," Cromwell and Parliament were having another violent quarrel. This may sound surprising, since the members of the Rump had been selected a few years before by Cromwell himself; but it is easily understood. Remember that this Parliament was really a continuation of the last one which Charles had called, and which could not be dissolved except by its own wish. As you can imagine, the members did not want to give up their pleasant jobs. A number of them were getting rich, as politicians sometimes do today, by secretly accepting "gifts" in return for political favors. Cromwell saw what was going on, and sternly disapproved.

He suggested that Parliament dissolve itself and hold new elections. But the members refused. The most that Cromwell could get from them was a promise to hold elections a few years later. As you can see, although Cromwell was the most important man in England, he was as yet by no means a dictator. Parliament still ruled the country. But he knew that the English people were now almost as dissatisfied with the new Parliamentary government as they had been with the dictatorship of Charles.

CROMWELL BECOMES DICTATOR

At first Parliament tried to get money to pay for its army and navy and wars by taking away the property of royalists and of the Anglican Church, and selling it to merchants and lawyers and owners of property who had supported the rebel cause. Many honest gentlemen were ruined as a result, and there was much indignation among the farmers and peasants. But even this harsh method did not provide enough money. Soon everybody in England was complaining of the government's high taxes.

Cromwell told Parliament that it no longer had the country's confidence, and again urged new elections. Reluctantly the members agreed—but only, they said, if they could be sure of being members in the next Parliament, without having to be elected. In other words, what they really wanted was to keep the same Parliament, with a few new members who would be elected.

This was an outrageous demand, and it infuriated Cromwell. He took several days to decide what to do. Finally he called a group of army officers to discuss the matter with the leaders of

Parliament. At this the members became frightened, and attempted to pass the unfair bill about the new elections before Cromwell should hear about it. But someone told him what was going on, and he took a squad of soldiers and rode to the House of Commons, as Charles once had ridden before him.

Leaving his soldiers outside, Cromwell entered and quietly took his seat while the uneasy members watched him. When a vote on the election bill was called for, he rose and began to speak. At first his voice was very low, but as he spoke, he became angrier and angrier, until finally his temper ran away with him, and he told the members exactly what he thought about them.

One member interrupted Cromwell to object to his "strange language . . . unusual in Parliament. . . . And from a trusted servant, too. . . ." This caustic remark gave Cromwell just the opportunity he was waiting for. "We have had enough of this!" he shouted. "I will put an end to your prating! It is not fit that you should sit here any longer. You shall now give place to better men. Call them in!"

His soldiers entered, and stood grimly silent, awaiting orders. Then Cromwell went on in his harsh voice, "You are no Parliament! I say you are no Parliament! Depart, I say, and let us have done with you. In the name of God—go!"

Then he picked up the mace which lay on the Speaker's table, and which was and is today the symbol of Parliament's authority. "What shall we do with this bauble?" he said aloud. He handed it to a soldier. "Take it away!" Like a flock of frightened sheep, the members crowded out through the great doors. Cromwell had become dictator of England.

GOOD-BY TO FREEDOM

Now you will notice a curious thing. Cromwell had just led a revolution in order to obtain freedom for the English people— freedom to make their own tax laws, freedom of worship. But as soon as he got rid of Parliament, he began to take away some of that freedom from the people. He did things which were tyrannical and cruel, and he became more and more ambitious for power.

As you will see many times in this book, even if a ruler sincerely wants to make life better for his people, it is dangerous for him to have absolute power. For power runs away with him. In order to keep it he has to do things that he never dreamed of— just about the same things that an entirely selfish ruler would do.

At first Cromwell did not admit that he was a dictator. He summoned another Parliament called the Parliament of Saints, for it was made up of very religious men, elected by the Independent churches of England. But these men knew nothing about making laws, and finally Cromwell, in disgust, sent them home. Then he called together a group of chosen supporters, and after "much seeking of God by prayer," they elected him to be dictator for life, with the title of "Lord Protector of the Commonwealth of England, Scotland, and Ireland." Many people cried out against him then, but he answered that he was only doing what had to be done for England's sake—to prevent further civil war. "God be judge," he told his critics, "between you and me."

Once he had absolute power, he did just what Charles had planned to do—he went to war against Spain. Owing to the English navy and Admiral Blake, the war was a great success, and England gained some new colonies. But it was very costly. Cromwell had to tax the business men of England more and more heavily, so that many of those who had formerly supported him became bitter. They began to plot against him with the royalist supporters of Prince Charles Stuart, the son of the dead King. Some religious fanatics and certain lovers of freedom who felt that Cromwell had betrayed them also conspired to kill him and start a new rebellion.

More and more as the people began to hate him, Cromwell had to rely on soldiers and spies to protect him. He set up a military government in England, so that everybody who dared oppose him could be sought out and punished. Judges had to interpret the laws of England to suit Cromwell, and if they did not, they were sent to prison. His dangerous enemies were hanged or beheaded, and many others were sent to the colonies to do the work of slaves. In other words, Cromwell, who had begun as a fighter for the freedom of the people, followed right in the footsteps of Richelieu, who had never cared at all about the freedom of the people.

CROMWELL TRIES TO BECOME KING

But Cromwell went Richelieu one better. Richelieu was loyal to his king, and Cromwell had no king. As time went on, it entered his mind that he himself ought to be the King of England.

In part, this was a matter of practical politics. He knew that the English people love a king, and he felt that his government would be stronger if he wore a crown and were called Oliver I. In addition, he very much wanted his son, Richard Cromwell, to succeed him as master of England. So he called another council of men who would obey him. Presently this obliging "Parliament" sent the Lord Protector Oliver Cromwell a "Humble Petition and Advice," urging him to become king and name his successor.

But now Cromwell hesitated. For he found that the army, which was his main strength, did not like the idea of having a king. Most of the soldiers had fought against King Charles, and they had no desire to see a substitute on his throne, not even their favorite general. Furthermore, many of them were opposed to royalty by religious teaching. They wanted "no King but God."

Cromwell dared not make enemies of his soldiers, especially while he was unpopular among the people. He decided to make friends of the business men and landowners. So he lowered their taxes a little, and gave many of them titles of nobility. Then he ended the unpopular military government, and permitted trial by jury, and did other things which the wealthier classes particularly approved. No doubt he hoped in this way to gain enough strength so that in spite of the army he could safely put on the crown of England. Whether or not this was a good scheme we will never know, for in the year 1658, in the midst of all these problems, he suddenly caught a chill, and died.

AND THEN—

With the remarkable man gone, England held its breath. Who would now govern? Richard Cromwell? Parliament? The army? The Stuart king? Richard was named Lord Protector, as Oliver had wished. He turned for aid to a properly elected Parliament. This suited the wealthy classes, who could control the elections, but it did not in the least please the soldiery. The army officers forced Richard to dissolve Parliament and finally to resign—which he did without much objection. He was a good-natured man, but not in the least a strong man; and he never really wanted to rule.

Then there was a period of confusion. No one knew what would happen next. Business became bad, as it always does in times of uncertainty, and the people were worse off than ever. The army officers who governed were so unpopular that they feared a new rebellion. Finally, by common consent, the Stuart prince was invited to take his father's place, and he became Charles II.

Thus, after years of war and death and terror and hardship, weary England was once more back where it had been under Charles I—with an extravagant king who had no respect for Parliament, and little tolerance for Puritans. But perhaps some good came out of it all, for the English learned a lesson at any rate. Thirty years later, there was another rebellion against the despotic Stuarts, and this time the people were wiser. Instead of getting rid of the crown altogether, they put it on the head of a Dutch prince who had royal English ancestors, and who knew how to get along with Parliament. Ever since then they have avoided serious rebellions by not letting either any one person, or any one Parliament, or any one party have too much power. This is the secret of democracy.

Frederick

Frederick Falls in Love with War

ON THE throne of Prussia, in the early 1700's, sat King Frederick William of the house of Hohenzollern, a burly, red-faced man with a violent temper.

Looking at the map of Europe, Frederick William would scowl. To the west were the great domains of France, whose young King Louis XV lived in splendor and luxury; and prosperous England, which could boast of ruling the seas. To the south was proud Austria, where Charles VI was styled Emperor, and had many ancient privileges. To the east was Russia, whose boy-Czar was master of a gigantic territory.

What was Prussia by comparison? Merely the largest among scores of little German kingdoms and dukedoms. Not a third the size of France in territory, population, or wealth. Not taken very seriously by the kings and ministers of the great powers. A poor country, so that the royal treasury was always having trouble collecting taxes. For an ambitious monarch, this was an intolerable state of affairs.

True, Frederick William was absolute ruler of Prussia. And he had an excellent army—small in comparison with those of France and Austria, but better drilled. Still he felt that fate had been unkind to Prussia and the Hohenzollerns.

To irritate the King still more, there was his son, young Prince Frederick. Here the royal scowl became fiercer. *Donnerwetter!* What was the matter with that boy? He did not act like a crown prince, and certainly not like a Hohenzollern. A disobedient and headstrong young fool! Instead of drilling with the army, he read books. Instead of riding and shooting, he played music to his mother and sister. Music! And the flute, of all instruments! Instead of studying affairs of state he studied Latin—against his father's orders, too! Instead of speaking German, like a simple Prussian gentleman, he preferred to speak French. And now it had come to the King's ears that the Prince had openly said that he despised German manners and customs. It was intolerable! What kind of king would the boy make for Prussia?

FATHER AND SON

Many times Frederick William had publicly scolded and punished his eighteen-year-old son, and it had done no good. But the King, like many stupid people, was determined to have his way at any cost. If a little punishment would not get results—then more punishment! That was how his mind worked.

But what punishment? A thought came to him. Young Frederick was very much in love with the Princess Amelia of England, and there was talk of a secret engagement. For political reasons the King had favored the marriage. But now he was too angry to think about politics. He would teach Frederick a lesson not soon to be forgotten!

He summoned the Prince to him, and in the presence of the Court, went into a violent outburst of rage. Insult followed insult, until the sensitive young man's face turned deathly pale, and he trembled with humiliation and resentment. Then in a final torrent of abuse the King forbade Frederick to think of marrying the Princess Amelia, or to correspond with her. Instead, he would have to marry some German princess, to be chosen for him.

When Prince Frederick left the court that day, he hated his father and knew that his father hated him. Gradually he made up his mind to leave his father's court—to run away. This was not at all a simple decision, such as the ordinary youth makes when his parents have treated him unjustly. Frederick had serious responsibilities to his country·and was an officer in the army. For him to run away meant to desert the army—an offense punishable by death or long imprisonment if he was caught, for the King would not be merciful. And if he escaped, then ever afterward he would be an exile from Germany, and could expect no money or help from any Prussian.

Nevertheless, Frederick was determined to risk it. He had two close friends, young army lieutenants named Katte and Keith, and to them he confided his plan. They agreed to aid him in getting to England, where he would find friends. One night, in the year 1730, while visiting a neighboring German kingdom, the three young men tried to mount their horses and quietly ride away. But a spy of the King's had discovered the secret, and at the last moment the Prince was surrounded by soldiers. Lieutenant Keith escaped, but Katte and Frederick were brought before the raging Frederick William.

THE LESSON

First his father deprived Frederick of his rank as crown prince. Then he was threatened with death, and finally turned over to a

court martial, which condemned him and Katte to imprisonment in a fortress.

But this did not pacify the King. If it had not been for his
wife and daughter, who begged him to spare the young Prince,
he would probably have had Frederick whipped in public if not
actually killed. But then he thought of another way to teach his
son a lesson.

One day several guards entered the room where Frederick was
confined and, seizing him by the arms, made him stand at the
window. In the stone courtyard below a masked executioner
came out, carrying his ax. The headsman's wooden block was
set up. In the midst of soldiers and officials a prisoner was led
forward. Sick with horror, Frederick tried to see who it was.
And then he saw. It was his friend Katte!

This was the King's revenge—that Frederick should stand and
see the gruesome death of his best friend, the gay Katte, whose
only crime was his love for his Prince, and whose life even the
court martial had spared.

Frederick screamed, struggled with his guards, and finally
fainted. But by the King's orders he was revived, and forced once
more to stand at the window, while Katte knelt, and the great
ax flashed in the air.

Later on Frederick found himself alone, lying on a cot. Surely
it had been a dream, a nightmare! His father could not be so
cruel! Slowly he got to his feet. The window drew him with an
irresistible fascination. Staggering, he moved forward until he
could look out. Then, with a cry, he buried his face in his hands.

For lying on the stone court in a pool of blood was the severed
head of poor Katte. The King had given orders that it be left

there, where his son could see it, so that the spectacle would not slip from his memory. Such was Frederick William's idea of "a lesson."

YOUNG FREDERICK SUBMITS

For days Frederick remained in his solitary room, seeing no one but his guards and the prison chaplain. Finally he could bear his loneliness no longer. He asked the chaplain how long he would have to stay there. "Forever," the chaplain answered sorrowfully. The word was like a blow. Frederick stared without speaking. Was this his fate—to remain for the rest of his life a prisoner, a prince of four walls? But the chaplain, watching him narrowly, went on, "Unless, of course, you obey the King's orders."

Frederick had vowed that he would never forgive nor ask forgiveness from his father. But now his weariness with prison life, his desire to walk and ride in the open air, and see his friends, and have good times—all this was stronger than his hatred. "What orders?" he asked.

The chaplain explained. The King had relented—a little—for Emperor Charles of Austria had pleaded that the young Prince be forgiven. If Frederick promised to obey his father in everything—if he agreed to give up all the foolish habits which the King disapproved—if he conducted himself henceforth like a Prussian soldier—if he would work hard from morning to night in the government offices—then he would be allowed to leave the fortress. But even then, until he had proved himself a dutiful son, he could not go outside the walls of the town where he was imprisoned.

With a sigh, Frederick submitted. A few days later his father sent a message of grim approval. "The whole town shall be his prison," wrote the King. "I will give him employment . . . But if he kicks or even rears again, he shall forfeit the succession to the crown, and perhaps . . . life itself."

Frederick no longer dared kick or rear. So obedient did he appear, such a good Hohenzollern did he become, that the King was delighted. A year later the Prince was allowed to return to Berlin and to wear a military uniform. He drilled on the parade grounds in Potsdam until even his father was satisfied. Another year, and the Prince was made colonel of a regiment. Then the King found him a German princess to be his bride. Frederick detested her, but he married her nevertheless. His father was actually affectionate to him now, and presented him with a large country estate.

Naturally, there was a great deal of hypocrisy in Frederick's attitude. He still hated Frederick William. Years later, when he was a middle-aged man, he would wake up at night in a cold sweat of fear, because he had been dreaming about his father. Nobody can go on for long pretending to be different than he is without changing, usually for the worse. And so it was with Frederick. Over the years he became another person. From being a warm-hearted, sensitive youth, he turned into a hard, suspicious, calculating man. He no longer had any real respect for his own feelings, or those of anyone else. Except for his mother and sister, he never really cared for anybody; and he despised the entire human race. Religion he considered a waste of time, suitable only for old women. He treated his wife brutally. But his father was pleased with him because he was "dutiful," and that was the important thing.

FREDERICK BECOMES KING

Frederick had, however, a very clever and even a brilliant mind, and he could talk on equal terms with the wisest and most amusing men in Germany. Voltaire, the great French writer, used to visit him and correspond with him—which was an honor, even for a king. This seemed to have a good effect on Frederick. Voltaire, and the other philosophers and writers whom he liked to see, were men of liberal ideas. They believed that kings should be careful of the interests of the common people, and should avoid unnecessary wars. Among the "intellectuals" it was fashionable to hold such beliefs, and Frederick wanted to be thought an intellectual, so he held them too. He even wrote some little books which made everybody say, "What a wonderful king he will be!"

But in his ideas about war as well as in his attitude toward his father, Frederick was insincere. In 1740 his father died, and he came to the throne. At once he forgot all the fine things he had told Voltaire and had written down. Now at last he was master of Prussia. He would show the world! He would do more than his father, with all his fierceness, had ever done!

There was no real reason for Frederick to go to war with anybody. Prussia was not a wealthy country, but the people got along well enough. Their chief complaint was that the King's officials interfered too much with their business affairs.

Men who go into business for themselves do so, of course, because they intend to make money. But they cannot make much money unless the government allows them a little freedom. In Frederick's time, if a man wanted to go into business, he had to get permission from some official, and this might take a long time, unless he gave the official a bribe. If he wanted to rent a house for his factory or shop, he had to get the government's permission again. And then it might turn out that the third cousin of some powerful baron wanted to go into the same business; so the baron would see to it that his cousin received permission, while the business man was refused. Besides, there were always the King's taxes, which were very high. And if a business were very profitable, then the King might decide to turn it into a royal monopoly—like Charles Stuart's soap business. Everything taken together, it was risky for a man with a little money to put it into a factory or a shop in Frederick's Prussia.

FREDERICK AND THE BUSINESS MEN

The kings of England in those days had learned that it was foolish to discourage business men in this way. They discovered that when many men went into business, the royal treasury was better off. You can see why this is so. If a man started a factory for making tin pans, for example, he had first to buy the tin, and this meant more money for the owner of the tin mine. Then the man would have to hire workmen to make the pans, and he would have to pay them—although of course he paid them as little as possible. The workmen would spend their money for bread and beer and cloth. This would give a larger profit to the landlord on whose land the grain was grown; and it would help the brewer who made the beer, and the owner of the mill where the cloth was woven. As a result the King's taxes on the tin pan factory and the mine, and the brewery and the farm and the mill, would bring in more money for his treasury.

In England these ideas were well understood, and it was becoming easier and easier for a man with a little money and a little energy to go into business for himself; and the King and lords and business men were all growing rich together. Even in some of the little German states near Prussia the kings and dukes were changing the old laws so as to encourage private business. But Frederick, like many other kings, was too interested in being famous and powerful to think much about business. Besides, if the business men became important, they would want a parliament so that they could help make the laws; and like Charles I, Frederick hated the idea of giving up any of his power, or of being criticized by his subjects.

So he continued to tell everyone in Prussia just what he had to do, and to punish him if he did not do it. He ran the entire country as if it were an army. He did not care whether the people were contented. He treated them just as his father had treated him. He told them that they had a Duty—to work to make Prussia great—and that nothing else, neither private happiness, nor family love, nor religion, must be allowed to interfere. By "Prussia," of course, he meant Frederick.

Years later, Frederick realized that the spirit of independence in his people had been nearly crushed, and he said in disgust, "I am tired of ruling over slaves." But he himself was more responsible than anyone else for the blind obedience of many Prussians to the orders of the state, and their need to be told exactly what to do. In some ways, he prepared the minds of the German people for what happened in Germany recently under Adolf Hitler.

WAR AND TRICKERY

Frederick's mind, then, was made up. He deliberately chose the path of "glory" and of power, instead of the path of peace and prosperity for his people. His father had left him a splendid army of 80,000 trained men. Good! The only question was, where should he strike first?

He knew that Austria was no longer the mighty empire it once had been; and on its throne now sat a woman, the Empress Maria Theresa. Frederick had little respect for women. Here was an opportunity. Without warning, he would seize the Austrian province of Silesia, which lay on his southern boundary. And if Maria Theresa "attacked him," then he would persuade the French, who had their own reasons for fighting Austria, to become his allies in the war.

Once he had written that it was criminal to conquer territory to which one had no lawful claim. But that was in the old days, when Voltaire had been his friend. And although Prussia had a treaty of friendship with Austria, what was a treaty? A scrap of paper. "When Prussia shall have made her fortune," he said cynically, "it will be time enough to give herself the appearance of keeping her promises."

Suddenly, then, he led his army into Silesia. To the frightened peasants he at first said that he was coming at the request of Maria Theresa. Soon he had occupied the entire country, and imprisoned the Austrian officials and policemen. Then he learned that the youthful Empress was not at all willing to be bullied. She had obtained from England a promise of help against France, and she was sending a powerful army to Silesia.

At the town of Mollwitz the Austrian army met the Prussians, and a great battle took place. At first the Prussian lines gave way, and Frederick, believing he was defeated, sprang on his horse and rode frantically north. Later, however, he heard to his astonishment that his army had rallied and scored a brilliant victory.

Presently Austria, attacked by France, decided to make peace with Prussia and give up Silesia. Frederick agreed, without even consulting his French allies. The result was that France was now left to face both Austria and England, and the French were furious at Frederick.

He spent the next two years in improving and enlarging his army. It had to be ready, he said, "down to the last button." Then he realized the Austrians were beating France, and that next they would probably try to take Silesia away from him. So he again entered the war against Austria.

This time the French tricked him as he had formerly tricked them. They withdrew their troops from his support. Now Frederick was in trouble. For a while it looked as if Maria Theresa's troops would drive him out of Silesia. But by this time he had become a skilful general, and he was able to win several victories against heavy odds. At last Maria Theresa wearily agreed to make peace with him again, and to let him keep the conquered territory.

PEACE

He had succeeded. He had done more, risked more, and gained more than his terrible father ever had. But his splendid army had been shattered, and his treasury was empty. He needed peace—for a while.

Some of the things that Frederick did in the years of peace that followed were helpful to the Prussian people. For instance, he forbade greedy lawyers to drag out lawsuits, as they were in the habit of doing so as to make their clients pay more money. He frightened corrupt judges so that they no longer dared take bribes. He made it possible for poor people to go to law when necessary, and to have a fair hearing. And he gave orders that the courts must no longer punish criminals by torturing them.

Then he made it easier for people to get married, and he said that everybody, no matter of what religion, would be welcomed in Prussia. And he helped some new industries get started by giving them money from the royal treasury.

But while he did a few things for the benefit of the people, he did others to their injury. He increased the army until it was so costly that taxes had to keep going up and up, and people were in despair. He bullied the judges so that it was sometimes impossible for them to be really fair in deciding law cases. And while pretending to be above religious prejudice, he persecuted the Jews so as to get whatever money they had. One of his favorite tricks was to make every Jew buy porcelain from the royal monopoly. But they could not buy what they wanted. They had to take what they were given, and pay whatever price was demanded. And they could not even keep what they bought, but had to send their porcelain out of the country.

EVERYTHING FOR THE ARMY

In other countries all over Europe, even in Austria, the serfs, the poorest farm laborers, who were virtually slaves on the farms of the noble landlords, had been freed and given certain rights. Frederick knew that as "a liberal and enlightened monarch" he should end serfdom in Prussia. But when he attempted to do so, the Junkers, as the Prussian aristocrats are called, grew angry. He dared not offend them, because all the officers of his army were Junkers. Naturally, he did not want to do anything that might weaken his wonderful army. So the serfs of Prussia continued to drag out their miserable lives in bondage.

In one way, it was an advantage to his beloved army if the peasants were miserable, because then they would not object so much when they were forced to become soldiers. The people respected the army, but they also hated it. The officers and sergeants were generally so brutal that if an ordinary soldier broke a minor rule of discipline, he would be kicked black and blue; and if he broke a serious rule, he might be cut to ribbons with a whip until he could not stand. Sometimes the Prussians would secretly raid the neighboring German states to seize poor peasants for the Prussian army, and they were so cruel that the angry rulers of those states offered rewards for "the bodies of Prussian recruiting sergeants, dead or alive."

Everything in Prussia was done so that the army would be strong. The stronger the army became, the poorer, and more miserable, the rest of the people became. This is what happens everywhere when a ruler tries to make his nation a great military power. Even the money that Frederick gave for business was not really intended to help the business men. It was for the army. He wanted new businesses so that Prussia could herself make most of the goods she needed, and would not have to import very much from other countries. For in wartime, of course, it might be impossible to import some things. Very recently Adolf Hitler also tried to make Germany "self-sufficient," but he was merely imitating Frederick.

Frederick had fallen in love with war, and he succeeded in turning Prussia for a while into a strong fighting nation. But we may well wonder what good that did most of his subjects.

GLORY

Before going to war again, the King decided to change his ally. France was no longer as strong as England, he believed, for their war in America was turning out unfavorably for the French. Therefore he turned away from France, and made an alliance with the English, who promised to send him a great deal of money.

At this France quickly joined in a new alliance with Austria, Russia, and the German state of Saxony. Naturally, when Frederick saw himself surrounded by enemies, he became alarmed and decided to strike before the other side was ready. Almost overnight he conquered Saxony and invaded Austrian territory. He was confident of success. The war would be short, he expected, and victory was certain. He announced that "The peaceful citizen is to notice no change when the country is at war."

He was mistaken. There came an unexpected victory by the Austrians. Then the Russians invaded Prussia. Next, the French entered a neighboring German state. Frederick found himself waging a desperate war of defense, which lasted for seven long years.

Now he showed that he was a man of courage and of iron will. Certainly, without him the Prussians could not have held off their enemies. He was everywhere, encouraging his men, instructing his generals, and sustaining hope. Yet as defeat followed defeat, he himself hardly dared to hope.

In the midst of this struggle his mother and favorite sister died —the only two women he had ever loved. This was a great grief to him. Tormented by his thoughts and by illness, he began to grow old before his time. Prussia came to know him as a thin, bent, gray little man in a faded, snuff-stained blue uniform— "old Fritz," his army affectionately called him.

Then he suffered another blow. While France had been sending her best soldiers to fight the Prussians, England had quietly gobbled up many of the French colonies in America. Now the English had nothing more to gain from the war, so they stopped giving Frederick money, which he badly needed. He was in despair, for he saw that he had helped to conquer America for England with Prussian blood, and he never forgave the English for their "treachery." But we must remember that England was only putting into practice Frederick's own idea, which we can sum up as "every nation for itself." It is this idea, by the way, which makes wars so frequent in the world's history.

Although Frederick was now fighting alone, he tightened his thin lips and repeated again and again, "I will conquer or perish with my army." Then luck came to his rescue. The Russians had a chance to capture Berlin, and when they missed it, Frederick was able to defeat them. Soon afterward a new Czar, who admired Frederick, came to the throne of Russia, and withdrew his armies from the war. Then England and France made peace, and persuaded Maria Theresa to end the fighting and sign a treaty with Frederick.

When the war ended, Frederick was called "the great," the "wonder of the world." For he had led a small nation against all the great powers of the continent, and had not lost. He became the most famous king of his time, and his army was considered the best in Europe.

WORK

Frederick had won glory. But in spite of that, he was a bitter and lonely man. He had only one thought—to work. For he realized that the war had ruined Prussia. In the city of Berlin one person out of every three was living on charity. If the people were not to starve, everybody would have to work harder than ever before.

"Work!" he told his people. "Work!" He himself would get up at five in the morning and work until late at night. And he would make his ministers, even the old men, work the same way. He treated these ministers just as harshly as he treated everybody else. He used to force them to stand up all day long because he said it made them think better—until one elderly statesman fell dead of exhaustion in a meeting of Frederick's council.

To the unhappy people of Prussia the King promised "a new creation." He promised to help business, and to make everybody prosperous. He began by borrowing a large sum of money from bankers. He owed this money to the employees of the government, who had not been paid for years. But when they asked for what was due them, he gave them only a little bit. The rest he handed out to business men and landowners, so that they could afford to hire more men to work for them. He also spent money to build new villages; for he had invited Poles and Bohemians to settle in Prussia, in order to increase the population. When you read later on about Adolf Hitler and his talk of a "pure German race," remember that less than two centuries ago one-sixth of all

Prussians were immigrants from Poland and Bohemia. The races of Europe are so mixed up nowadays that there is no such thing as a "pure" race.

The things that Frederick did for business helped those who owned property of some kind, and provided jobs for many others. But most of the people continued to be very poor. And business men still complained that they could do nothing without permission. They made a bitter little joke about it: "We are very lucky, because among us everything is done by the King."

No sooner was business a little better than Frederick went right back to his old practice of squeezing the country for the benefit of the army. From the 80,000 men he had started with, he now made an army of 200,000. He made everyone pay taxes on everything he bought, until the people groaned. And finally he stopped giving any of the tax money back to help business, or to build schools, or to feed the poor, because he wanted to keep it in the treasury "for the next war."

"NO ONE WAS SAD"

The taxes made the King very unpopular. Everybody in Prussia was grumbling. The people especially resented Frederick's coffee monopoly, for he forbade them to buy coffee except at the royal mills, where they had to pay three times as much as in the past. The Prussians were very fond of coffee, so they used to smuggle it in from Austria, where they could buy it much cheaper. Finally Frederick realized that most of the coffee being drunk in Prussia was smuggled, and that he was not getting his profit. In a great rage he gave orders that spies should go out everywhere and search all houses where they thought they would find smuggled coffee, and arrest the people who drank it. The people called these spies "coffee smellers," hated them, and invented a hundred ways to fool them.

If this had happened in England, there certainly would have been riots and even rebellion, as in the days of King Charles.

Even the Prussian people, who had been trained to put up with almost anything from their King, were not as loyal as they had been. Shortly before his death, Frederick sent an army into Bavaria, in an unimportant little war. He was horrified to find that his soldiers were deserting by the hundreds. In all the misery of the Seven Years' War few of his troops had deserted, but now they were no longer reliable.

As his troubles increased, Frederick blamed his ministers. But actually he was responsible, because his ministers did only what he told them to. He had taken the last shreds of freedom away from his people. When he died, in 1786, someone wrote from Berlin that "everything was as still as death, but no one was sad."

Frederick believed that absolute monarchs would continue to rule as they wished, all over Europe. If he had lived a few years longer, he would have learned otherwise. After him his nephew, Frederick William II, came to the throne. The people demanded that taxes be reduced, and the new King, who was anxious to be popular, agreed. Instead of making the people pay, he decided to take his money out of Frederick's "war chest." In a few years the treasury was empty.

Then, in 1789, the great French Revolution burst on the world. Prussia sent troops to help crush the rebels. But to everybody's astonishment, the French defeated them. For untrained as the revolutionary soldiers were, they believed in their cause, and were willing to die for it, while the disciplined Prussians had lost their spirit.

This was the beginning of Prussia's decline, which—as you will read in the next chapter—led for a while to some very dark days indeed. We can see now that in making Prussia dangerous to her neighbors Frederick had slowly weakened the loyalty of his oppressed people; until at last the government crumbled from within. This is a lesson well worth remembering for our own times.

Napoleon

Napoleon Tries to Conquer Europe

O
F ALL the soldiers and statesmen who have lived in recent centuries, none is so famous as Napoleon Bonaparte. But although everybody knows his name, and that he was the most powerful ruler of his day, surprisingly few people can tell you how he got his power. To many it seems almost as if there was something magical about it—that one day he was poor and unimportant, and the next he was great and powerful, like Aladdin. But Napoleon had no Genie of the Lamp to perform miracles for him. True, his success came swiftly, but it was the result of shrewdness and ability, and hard work, and good luck—like the success of less famous men. He had his ups and downs, his disappointments, and moments of despair. More than once before he was twenty-five years old, he considered himself ruined and a failure.

As a boy, Napoleon was clever, but hot-tempered and something of a bully. He grew up in a large family, which was run with an iron hand by his mother. She was a very strong-minded woman, and it is from her, no doubt, that Napoleon inherited his own strength of will. Many times in his youth she gave him a beating for disobedience, using a stout switch. Even when he was sixteen, he was not too old to be whipped when he angered her.

He grew up, not on the soil of France, but in the Mediterranean island of Corsica, which had just a little while before been seized by France. The French governor of Corsica wanted to do a favor for Charles Bonaparte, Napoleon's father, who was a lawyer; so he arranged to send the second Bonaparte son, Napoleon, to a French military school, where he could learn to become an army officer.

He was a pale, thin, studious youth, who showed no sign of future greatness, except, perhaps, in his remarkable memory. His favorite study was history, and especially the history of great wars. Mathematics also appealed to him strongly, and this fact enabled him to become a good artillery officer; for, of course, the accurate aiming of cannon demands a knowledge of mathematics.

THE REVOLUTION

By 1789, he had become a lieutenant of the lowest rank. In that year the great French Revolution broke out, and King Louis XVI was forced to accept a parliament, which began to make new laws for the country. This parliament, which the French called the National Assembly, was a good deal like the British House of Commons in Cromwell's time. It was composed largely of middle-class property owners—lawyers, landholders, and merchants. The first thing they did was to take away the lands and money of the Catholic Church and the nobility.

This caused a great outcry among the aristocrats of all the countries of Europe. The kings of England and Prussia, and the Emperor of Austria were furious at the French. They were afraid that such an example might encourage their own subjects to revolt. So they sent armies to help King Louis get back his power.

However, the French troops were full of enthusiasm for the new government, and fought so bravely that even the famous Prussian army gave way before them.

As always in such disturbed times, a number of different political parties sprang up in France, each trying to get for itself the power which the King had lost—the power to collect taxes, and make laws, and give orders to the army, and draw salaries from the government. There was a royalist party which wanted to give the power back to the King and the Church. This party was made up mostly of frightened aristocrats and priests, many of whom soon fled from the country. There was a middle-class republican party, most of whom wanted to get rid of the King, and let the Assembly of business men and lawyers go on making the laws. There was a strong radical party, which wanted to do away with King and aristocrats and Church and give all power to a new Assembly, which would be elected by the votes of all the people, whether or not they owned property.

Napoleon, like a great many other young men, was a radical. He was full of hope that France would become a country where everybody was free and equal, and all men were brothers, property or no property. He even wrote a little essay about it. Years afterward, when someone showed him this essay, he threw it in the fire.

But for a while he was too worried about his family back home in Corsica to play much part in politics. A revolution against the French government had broken out on the island, and the property of the Bonapartes was taken away. The entire family had to fly for their lives to France, where they were all poor and thoroughly miserable.

Napoleon was not only discontented on his family's account,

but on his own, for he was already a tremendously ambitious young man. To be a mere lieutenant was intolerable for him. But he knew that before he could hope to be promoted, he would have to catch the eye of the politicians who ran the army. With this purpose, he wrote another pamphlet on politics, supporting the radicals, or Jacobins, as they were called. He sent the pamphlet to a few influential men of that party whom he knew slightly, and they liked it. This was a clever move, for it made the politicians pay attention to Napoleon, whom they might otherwise never have noticed.

FRANCE BEGINS A WAR

Presently King Louis and his lovely but feather-pated Queen, Marie Antoinette, tried to run away from France, so that they could lead a royalist army against the liberals and radicals. They were caught, tried, and executed by the angry republicans. At this the other kings of Europe became furious all over again, and talked about sending new armies to attack France, and of putting the King's brother on the throne.

Strange as it may seem, the business men's party in France, which then controlled the Assembly, actually wanted a war. Owing to the great uncertainty of the times, business was very bad. They hoped war would help them get more money for their goods and grain. Besides, the radical Jacobins wanted to put heavy taxes on the business men; and the business men thought that if the country was fighting foreign enemies, the Jacobins would keep quiet. So they voted in the Assembly to declare war without waiting to be attacked; and although many radicals objected, France sent an army against Austria.

This was lucky for Napoleon. At the time he was in danger of being court-martialed as a deserter, for he had taken a leave of absence, and had stayed away too long. However, the outbreak of war meant that France needed all her officers, and Napoleon's superiors knew that he was an expert on artillery. Instead of being punished, he was forgiven and promoted to be a captain.

The war turned out to be a mistake for the business men and property owners of France. The first battles went against the French troops. Then there was a shortage of food, and some peasants revolted, demanding that the throne and Church be restored. Finally the Assembly in Paris was invaded by fierce mobs of poor people, who drove most of the members of the business men's party out of the Assembly. After that the radicals gained control and began to govern the country.

The first laws passed by the Jacobins almost ruined everybody who still had any money or property. This caused new revolts. In several parts of France, business men, aristocrats, and peasants together seized towns and cities and demanded that France be given a king again. So the republican Jacobin government had to send troops not only against the Austrians, but also against its own cities.

NAPOLEON GETS HIS CHANCE

One of these royalist centers was Toulon, in the south of France. The republican army had trouble in recapturing the city, and it was decided that a good artillery officer was needed to help in the siege.

The war department of the radical government looked over the list of artillery officers. Someone recommended Captain Bonaparte. It was pointed out that this Bonaparte had written a little pamphlet which showed that he supported the Jacobins. The powerful Robespierre himself, who was the leader of the Jacobins, had seen this pamphlet and approved it. And not only was young Bonaparte a radical and a patriot, but he was also an able officer.

In this way, he was selected for the post, his first real opportunity. For a while he made little progress, for the general in command at Toulon did not agree with his ideas about the way to use artillery. But at last there was a change in generals. The new commander saw the wisdom of Napoleon's plans, and adopted them. Toulon quickly fell to the republican army.

The government was delighted, and since the general gave Napoleon a good share of the credit, the war department decided to reward the young captain. Owing to the shortage of officers, promotions were rapid in those days, and Napoleon's politician friends were again working for him. No one was very surprised when the rank of brigadier general was given to the young man.

NAPOLEON IS RUINED

To be a general at the age of twenty-five sounds like success, but the ambitious Napoleon was far from satisfied. He was more mature in mind than most men are at forty; and he still had to obey the orders of other generals who, he knew, were far less talented than he. First they ordered him to join a French army in Italy, which then belonged to Austria. But when he got there, he was given nothing to do. Then he was sent around France to inspect fortresses. Then back to Italy, again in a minor post. He began to wonder whether he would ever get any farther.

Meanwhile, the Jacobin leader Robespierre had been growing

unpopular. The price of bread was very high, nobody had any money, the army was losing, and everybody was frightened. To keep the people quiet, Robespierre and the extreme radicals had been killing their opponents, cutting off their heads on the guillotine, or shooting them by hundreds. Finally the country grew sick of all this horrible butchery. A part of the radical party led by a man named Carnot revolted, and Robespierre himself was arrested and executed on the guillotine.

This story of the French Revolution shows that when people are miserable, it is very hard for any government to stay in power. Because there was hunger and poverty throughout France, the liberals and radicals together had taken power from the royalists. But times continued bad, so the liberals and radicals had quarreled, and the radicals had taken power from the liberals. That did not help the people either; so now the radicals quarreled among themselves, and the Carnot party took the power away from the Robespierre party.

Naturally, when Robespierre fell from power everybody who had supported him was in danger. Napoleon was actually arrested. But some of his political friends were on the side of the new leader, Carnot, and they persuaded Carnot to release him.

The war department, however, now regarded young General Bonaparte with suspicion, and he was removed from Italy. Another royalist rebellion among starving peasants in western France had broken out, and Napoleon was ordered to go there and suppress it. He had too much respect for the honor of his profession, however, to enjoy shooting down unarmed peasants, and he refused. Thereupon he was reprimanded and dropped from the list of active officers.

It seemed as if his career was ruined. In the first place, he had no money. To pay his rent he had to sell his books and watch. For a time he thought of offering his services as a general to the Sultan of Turkey. (Remember how Cromwell thought of going to Germany when things were bad for him.) Then the young man coldly planned to marry a wealthy widow for her money. When she refused him, he was furious with her. He was not a very romantic figure. His body was short and his face, at that time, was very thin and bony. He had caught malaria in Italy, which made his skin yellow, and some trouble with his scalp had forced him to shave his head.

LUCK CHANGES AGAIN

So with bitterness in his heart he stayed in Paris. Still, he was careful to pay calls on important people. Finally the wife of one politician took an interest in him, and persuaded her husband to have Napoleon given another chance. Again he was ordered to join the French army fighting the Austrians in Italy. But this time, too, he failed to distinguish himself, and once more he was sent back to Paris, with no work to do.

That was the luckiest thing that could have happened to him. Just then the royalists were plotting to revolt against Carnot's government, for they knew that the people were still as discontented as ever. When the revolt began, it looked for a time as if the royalists would capture Paris. The republicans were in a panic. They assembled all the troops they had nearby, but could not decide whom to select for a general.

One of the important politicians knew about Bonaparte's work at Toulon, and recommended him. Carnot agreed, and Bonaparte was given the command. He had no trouble whatever. Issuing rapid orders to his troops, he quickly defeated the royalists in a street battle. In less than a day the revolt was crushed.

This victory made Napoleon a hero. The government was so relieved and so grateful that it made him commander-in-chief of a new army to be sent to Italy. And another widow—without money, it is true, but very beautiful—consented to marry the young general, who had fallen madly in love with her. Later, she was to become the Empress Josephine; and in time she would be divorced and cast aside by her ruthless husband.

A month after his marriage, Napoleon led 30,000 republican troops over the Alps into Italy. They were ragged, starving, cold, and short of ammunition. But they had courage and the greatest general of modern times to lead them. Nothing could stop him or them. He smashed the Austrians in a bloody battle, and before they had recovered, he smashed them again, and again, and again. In a year the Austrians were completely beaten, and northern Italy belonged to France.

One phrase which Napoleon used at this period hints at the changes taking place in his own thoughts about himself. When he was giving instructions about the new government of Italy, he did not say in concluding, "Such is the will of the French Republic." He said, instead, "Such is my will!" These were very royal words indeed in the mouth of a republican soldier.

NAPOLEON WORKS TO BE POPULAR

While Napoleon was winning his great victories, the other French generals were not doing much, so naturally he became more and more of a hero at home. The common people, as well as the soldiers, spoke of him affectionately as "the little corporal."

The most important statesmen in France corresponded with him frequently, and came to respect his ideas. Others were afraid of him, and envious.

The government at Paris was in trouble again. The owners of property disliked Carnot, for he was still too much of a radical for them. He made them lend money to the government, and they knew they would probably never get it back. Some of the politicians of the old liberal party, particularly two shrewd men named Sieyès and Talleyrand, wanted to get rid of Carnot and the National Assembly, and set up a new kind of government that business men and landowners would like—not with a king, but with a dictator who would keep the poorer people quiet.

Sieyès and Talleyrand did not feel strong enough to overthrow the republic themselves. They wanted another to help them— someone like Napoleon. They felt that his popularity with the people and the army might be very useful to them when the time came to act against Carnot and the Assembly.

Napoleon suspected what they had in mind. By this time he had lost most of his radical ideas about "liberty, equality, and fraternity." By nature he was a selfish man, and he was in favor of any government in which he would be important. If the business men's party was going to be the strongest, then he would be friendly to their side. But whatever happened, he knew that his popularity was his greatest advantage. So he was very careful to endear himself to the army and the people at every opportunity.

When the war in Italy ended, even though he was victorious, he was not altogether pleased. He feared that after Austria made peace and he returned to Paris the people would soon forget his triumphs. Reputations always are brighter at a distance.

Napoleon wanted another war, because so long as there was

war, he would be the most important and popular man in France.

WAR WITH ENGLAND

He knew how to start another war. At that time, the Low Countries—Belgium and Holland—belonged to Austria. These countries have always been—and still are—of great importance to England, for they lie on the English Channel. While they were held by a feeble empire, like Austria, the English did not worry very much. But if they became the property of a growing military power, like France, then England might be invaded without warning at any time. If France took the Channel countries away from Austria, England was bound to fight. So when the Austrians asked for peace, Napoleon insisted that they yield not only Italy, but also the Netherlands, to France. Austria had no choice but to agree.

The French people thought this was a wonderful gain, and praised Napoleon more than ever. If they had realized that the new territories meant a war with England, however, they would not have been so happy. For they, too, were tired of war. Some men who understood what was happening actually tried to hold a public meeting in Paris to explain it to the people, and to urge that the Netherlands be made an independent country. But the friends of Napoleon were on the watch for just such a move, and broke up the meeting. For they knew that he wanted war with England.

MORE POPULARITY

When the war began, many Frenchmen thought that Napoleon ought to take an army over the Channel and invade England right away. But he was too clever to do anything of the kind. England had a mighty navy, and could prevent the French troops from landing. Until the French could win on the sea, such an invasion was out of the question.

Napoleon had another plan, a fascinating plan. He would do something no one else had ever done since the days of ancient Rome. He would take an army to the East, and conquer Egypt and Western Asia. He would win a great colonial empire for France. And in so doing, he would close off the British trade route to India. This would greatly damage the profits of English business men.

Furthermore, Napoleon knew that while he was gaining new glory under the eyes of the Sphinx, his brother Lucien Bonaparte would look after things in Paris, and make sure that Sieyès and Talleyrand did not try to do anything without him.

So he talked the government into giving him an army and ships, and he sailed for Africa. By good luck—for a British fleet was nearby—he reached Egypt in safety. As usual, he immediately won several victories. And he enjoyed himself by posing as a great conqueror. He made some very stirring speeches to his army, including one under the Pyramids, beginning with the famous words: "Soldiers, from these Pyramids forty centuries look down on you."

But presently the English fleet found Napoleon's fleet, and destroyed it; and this defeat was fatal to his dream of conquest. For it meant that he could not obtain supplies or reinforcements. From this point on, although he conquered Egypt for a short time, and won battles in Syria, he really gained nothing for France. The chief result of all his marching and brilliant generalship was the slaughter of some thousands of young Frenchmen, Englishmen, and Egyptians.

Finally, owing to the lack of supplies, his army was in serious danger. Napoleon did not like the situation in the least. He had been sending reports to France about his wonderful victories. If he were to be defeated now, all his popularity might vanish over-night. Besides, he heard from brother Lucien that the political situation in France was very serious, and the royalists were trying again to restore the monarchy. Napoleon, said Lucien, had better come home.

So he left his army behind him to get along as best it could, and boarded a small boat, which slipped through the British fleet and brought him to France. When the word spread that he had landed, all the republicans were overjoyed. With the great General Bonaparte back, people felt that the royalists would never dare to rebel—that the republic was saved.

As he rode toward Paris, people turned out by the thousands to cheer him. Sieyès, who had become the most important statesman of the moment, sent for Lucien Bonaparte. "The die is cast," he said. "It is around your brother that we must rally." He meant that the time had come to overthrow the republic and set up a dictatorship.

NAPOLEON BECOMES DICTATOR

The first thing that had to be done, Sieyès and Napoleon agreed, was to close up the republican parliament, and give themselves the right to make the laws of France. But this was not easy, because in Paris many people still believed that a republic was desirable. The only solution was to get the parliament out of Paris, to prevent the people from rising to its defense, and then close it up. After that the popular Napoleon could explain his reasons to the people, and win them over.

So Sieyès pretended that he had discovered a great royalist plot against the Assembly, and persuaded the members to go for safety to a suburb of Paris. Then Napoleon took some troops. which were loyal to him personally, and, like Cromwell, declared the parliament dissolved, and made the members go home.

As a matter of fact, this was not quite so easy as it sounds, for when he started to address the members, they grew furious, and threatened him, and he became so upset that he could not go on with his speech. And the soldiers were not quite sure whether or not they loved Napoleon enough to overthrow the republic for him. If it had not been for Lucien Bonaparte, the plan might have failed. At the crucial moment Lucien shouted to the troops, "I swear that I will run my brother through with my sword, should he ever dare to threaten the liberties of France!" The soldiers believed him, and drove out the members of the Assembly. Sieyès and Napoleon then announced a new government, with themselves at its head.

Sieyès thought that he would supply the brains of the new government, while Napoleon supplied the popularity and the military successes. But he soon found that Napoleon liked his own brains best; and Sieyès did not dare oppose the man who controlled the army. Shortly Napoleon had made Sieyès a mere figurehead, and was dictator of France, with the title of First Consul.

FRANCE APPROVES

Napoleon was a wonderfully energetic ruler. He swiftly gave France a new constitution, and an excellent code of laws. He put into effect a new centralized tax system, which brought more money to the treasury at Paris. He pleased the business men and landowners by showing respect for their property rights. He made sure that all the officials of the government were loyal to him.

Then, like Richelieu, he organized a powerful secret service to seek out his enemies, and to prevent plots against him. Many royalists and Jacobins were arrested, some killed. Finally, when Napoleon felt that he was reasonably secure at home, he turned his attention once more to the war with Engand.

He still did not have a navy large enough for an attack on the island country. The British had given money to Austria, to help that weakened Empire raise another army against her ancient enemy, France. So Napoleon once more turned his attention to Austria. Of course, he did not dream of restoring peace to Europe, which he might have done by withdrawing from the Netherlands. To do so would have lessened his precious popularity, for the French people had by now been told so often the Netherlands were "rightfully" theirs that they believed it.

Napoleon announced it was necessary to fight Austria "in self-defense." He asked the people of France to vote whether they approved of him or not. And of course, almost everybody voted "yes," many because they really were full of admiration for him, and others because they were afraid to vote "no." Modern dictators, too, use these special votes of approval, or plebiscites, to show that they are acting "by the will of the people." Actually, plebiscites mean very little. Even if the people in their calm moments do not really approve of the dictator's actions, they are usually too excited by his speeches, and too afraid of his spies, to vote against him.

NAPOLEON BECOMES EMPEROR

In 1800, then, Napoleon led an army into Austria, and, as usual, won some great victories. Again Austria was compelled to surrender. England became frightened, and agreed to a truce, leaving the Netherlands to France if Napoleon would give up French claims to Egypt. Napoleon was perfectly willing. Although thousands of Frenchmen had died in winning Egypt, that country was of little value to France, while the Netherlands produced a great deal of profitable trade for the French business men who supported Napoleon and lent him money.

The French people were overjoyed. The war had cost the lives of many young men, and had made food expensive, while the wages of the people who worked on farms and in factories and shops were very low. They wanted peace, and when Napoleon gave them a victorious peace, they thought he was the greatest man who had ever lived.

Then Napoleon, seeing that he was more popular than ever, called one of those imitation parliaments which dictators like, and told it to appoint him Consul for life, with the right to name his successor—just like Cromwell. But, like Cromwell again, Napoleon was still not satisfied. He was king in everything but name; and he wanted the name, too. It annoyed him that when the kings of Europe wrote him letters they addressed him simply as "Monsieur," or "Sir"; while their letters to each other began "Monsieur my brother." Besides, he wanted to have a son who would inherit the throne of France. He dreamed of a Europe ruled by Bonapartes.

So he told his parliament to ask him to be Emperor of the French, "by the will of the people"; and then he graciously accepted the offer. He even made the Pope come from Rome to be present at the coronation. The French people love parades and grand ceremonies, and they were used to kings. Most of them applauded when Napoleon, who had always called himself a republican, suddenly changed into an Emperor. And those who wanted to grumble did not dare.

THE PRIDE OF AN EMPEROR

The English, of course, were not really content to have the French on the English Channel, especially since they knew Napoleon was building a big fleet. So again they sent money to Prussia and Austria, and again war got under way.

An incident occurred at this time which suggests the kind of man Napoleon had become. He had told his admiral that on a certain day he would review the new fleet, which was to sail down the bay. That day, a fierce storm came up, which made safe navigation impossible. When Napoleon appeared for the review, the fleet was still at anchor.

With flashing eyes he turned on the admiral, and demanded, "Why did you not obey my orders?"

The admiral replied, "Your Majesty can see that for yourself. You would not needlessly risk brave lives in such weather."

"Sir," cried Napoleon, his face pale with anger, "I have given you an order! The consequences are no concern of yours. Do what you are told!"

The admiral looked out at the great waves and howling winds, and shook his head stubbornly, "Sire, you ask the impossible! I cannot obey."

Napoleon looked as if he could not believe his ears. Then, with a cry, he raised the short riding whip that he carried. The admiral took a step backward and, biting his lip, put his hand on the hilt of his sword. A hush of horror fell on the other officers. After an instant the Emperor mastered himself, and said harshly, "You will leave the country at once and go to Holland. You no longer command here."

He then turned to another admiral, and gave orders that the review be held as planned. As soon as the ships began to sail across the bay it was seen that Napoleon had made a terrible mistake. Boat after boat capsized in the storm, and soon the beach was littered with the bodies of drowned seamen. Two hundred men perished, and a large part of the fleet was badly damaged.

When a dictator's pride runs away with his judgment, it is a very bad sign for the future. Of course, it is possible that Napoleon really did not realize the danger to the fleet, for he never understood the sea very well. But there can be no doubt that his vanity at this time could not bear even the slightest contradiction.

The same thing was true when he played games, such as chess. If he did not win, he became furious. The best chess players would always make it a point to let him beat them, so as not to incur his displeasure.

THE EMPIRE GROWS—

He had planned to invade England in 1805. But owing to various misfortunes to his fleet, he had to give up the idea. Instead, he turned around and marched once more against Austria. In the brilliant battle of Austerlitz he smashed a great Austrian army.

Then he continued on to meet the Prussian army, which still had a great reputation, from the days of Frederick the Great; and he won another decisive victory at Jena. The spirit of Prussia had been weakened by the harsh government of the Hohenzollerns, and after this one defeat the Prussian people did not care to go on fighting. Many of them, especially the business men, were even glad when Napoleon came to Berlin, and the Prussian King fled.

But they soon changed their tune. Napoleon broke up Prussia, and humiliated the people. He made them pay him a huge tribute, and taxes even heavier than they had paid to their own King. Soon they hated him and all the French. They began to dream of having their Hohenzollern back, and revenging themselves on France. In a later chapter you will read about their revenge.

—AND STILL THE EMPIRE GROWS

About this time, Napoleon suffered a severe loss, when his navy, which had cost him so much money, was destroyed by a British fleet under the great Admiral Nelson, at Trafalgar. That battle ended his hopes of competing with England on the seas. So he made another plan. He would injure the British business men where it hurt most—in the pocketbook. How? By "a continental blockade of British goods"—by not permitting anybody in Europe to buy anything from England or sell to England—by destroying British trade in Europe. Of course, to enforce such a blockade he would first have to conquer all Europe. But he believed that he could do it, and in this way bring England to her knees.

He began by defeating a Russian army which had come to the aid of Prussia. After that the Russian Czar agreed to stop trading with England. Then Napoleon drove the King of Spain from his throne, and made his own brother Joseph Bonaparte king in his place. Another brother, Louis, was already King of Holland, and a brother-in-law was King of Naples. It looked as if Napoleon's dream of a Europe ruled by Bonapartes was coming true. He was so intent on having a royal family that he forced one of his brothers to divorce his wife so as to marry a princess chosen by Napoleon.

Actually, although France seemed to be winning the war, her doom was near. England was so alarmed by the alliance between France and Russia that she determined at last to send English troops, as well as English money and ships, against Napoleon. And England was still rich and unhurt by war, whereas France had been impoverished, and had lost the flower of her young men. It is said that Frenchmen were taller, on the average, before Napoleon ruled France, than they have ever been since; because so many millions of tall, strong young men were killed in his battles before they could marry and have children.

THE EMPIRE COLLAPSES

Suddenly the tide turned against Napoleon. A revolt broke out in Spain, with English troops aiding it, and a French army was defeated. Napoleon's own brother in Holland refused to end Dutch trade with England, and had to be removed from his throne in consequence. The Pope objected to Napoleon's actions, so Napoleon imprisoned him; and this turned Catholics everywhere against him. Austria entered the war again, and two costly battles were required to beat her.

Then the Czar of Russia who had hoped that he and Napoleon would divide up Turkey, became doubtful of the French power, and decided to trade again with England. This was a fatal blow to Napoleon. Angrily he decided to invade Russia—otherwise his idea of a continental blockade of England was ruined. In 1812, he led a great army deep into Russia, as far as Moscow. But the cold and the snow and lack of food defeated him. Most of his army perished miserably, and he was forced to hasten back to France to raise new troops. True, he was encouraged when the United States made war against England, but this proved to be of little advantage to France.

The French people were rapidly becoming alarmed and dissatisfied. Napoleon tried to keep up their spirits with reports of imaginary victories, but they saw through these lies. "False as an army report" became a proverb throughout France. Clearly, Napoleon was not invincible after all. Clever politicians like Talleyrand began to prepare for the fall of the Empire, and to make private arrangements with the old royalists.

Hoping to make an ally of Austria, Napoleon had divorced his aging wife Josephine, of whom he had long since grown tired, and married an Austrian princess. But that did not prevent Austria from fighting him again, this time with Prussia and Russia as allies. In a great battle at Leipzig they defeated the French armies, and France lost all her German conquests at one blow. Then they pursued Napoleon into French territory.

NAPOLEON ABDICATES

The French business men were now as eager to get rid of Napoleon as they had once been eager to have him. He was making them "lend" him all their money, just as the old radical government had. As a matter of fact, Napoleon now tried to win support from the radicals, and to talk again about "the glorious revolution," and the rights of the common man to "liberty, equality, and fraternity."

But it was too late for such tricks. The Allies were on his heels. His armies were now made up of the last youth of France, many of them mere children. "If I must," cried Napoleon, "I shall arm the women!" Somehow he managed to win some more amazing victories. To the army and the people he made impassioned speeches, in which he cried dramatically, "Should Paris be taken, I shall no longer go on living!" But it was no use. Too many Frenchmen had died and been crippled. France did not have enough cannon fodder for him. The Allies entered Paris. And Napoleon decided not to commit suicide, after all.

Instead, he surrendered, and gave up his claim to the French throne. There was nothing else to do. He was allowed to retire to the little island of Elba in the Mediterranean, which was given to him to rule as he pleased. Europe breathed a sigh of relief. The royalists put King Louis XVIII on the throne, with Talleyrand as his chief minister. The French aristocrats agreed to forget the old feudal ways and to accept the "capitalism" that had been growing up since Richelieu's day. "Capitalism" is the name for a way of life in which the government allows business men to buy and sell and invest and make money if they can without much interference. To have capitalism, a country needs a parliament to make laws which business men and property owners approve; and Louis XVIII was quite willing to accept such an arrangement.

WATERLOO

Napoleon had been master of Europe. He was still a young man, as rulers go. Could he be content now with a few square miles of barren land? Never. That great ambition was in him still. To the dismay of Europe's kings, he suddenly escaped and reappeared in France. He knew how to touch the hearts of the French people. They had been glad to get rid of him a few months earlier, but when they saw the famous "little corporal" again, when they heard his magic words and promises of good things to come, they flocked to his banner as if hypnotized. His old army officers rushed to join him. Almost overnight he raised an army. As he entered Paris, King Louis XVIII and Talleyrand fled for safety. For a little while it looked as if the Empire of the Bonapartes was to be restored.

He wrote the kings of Europe, asking for peace. But England would have none of him. Instead they sent an army under the Duke of Wellington, while Prussia, too, rushed troops to the border. On June 18, 1815, the armies met in Belgium, at Waterloo —and that was the end of Napoleon's dream.

This time the English took no chances. They sent him to St. Helena, a little island in the Atlantic, from which there could be no escape. And so, at the age of forty-five, his astonishing career was over.

The man who had been master of Europe turned into a bored and unhappy victim of his own memories. One night, while playing chess with a friend, he said, "What time is it?"

"Midnight, sire," the friend replied.

"Good," said Napoleon bitterly.

"Why 'good,' sire?"

"Because I have won another victory over time. There is one day the less for me to live."

THE POWER OF A NAME

But even as a prisoner, Napoleon still was able to do a remarkable thing. He made a legend of himself. He dictated some books to his friends, in which he told what he had done, and his reasons. In these books, he made himself appear to be a wonderful man. He spoke of himself as a friend of the poor, "a crowned Washington" who had wanted to help the oppressed peoples of Europe, but had been prevented by the greed and envy of kings. He did not write anything, of course, about the millions who had died in his wars, and the other millions who had gone hungry, and about the thousands who had spent years in prison because they did not like him. He even had the audacity to say that his Empire was "a kind of republic." He said that France would some day turn again to a Bonaparte to rule her, and he referred to his young son, who had gone to Austria to live, and who died young, as Napoleon II.

And as time went on, France, instead of laughing at Napoleon, or cursing him, actually began to believe him. He became the hero of a kind of fairy tale, in which his wars were glorious and wonderful. People felt that all the Frenchmen who had suffered for him really should have been glad of the chance. Children sang little songs about how wonderful he was. At his death in 1821 the whole world was tremendously stirred.

The legend grew. Although people in France were better off than they had been under the Empire, they sighed for "the old days, the old deeds," the romantic times of the great Napoleon. Every old soldier of the Napoleonic "Grand Army" was regarded as a hero, and poets and authors wrote hundreds of songs and books telling how these men had "drunk death like wine."

So deeply did the French come to love the memory of Napoleon that when hard times came again, in 1848, they turned to his nephew, Louis Napoleon Bonaparte, and made him President of the French Republic. And like his uncle, Louis Napoleon soon got rid of the republic and made himself Napoleon III, Emperor of the French. Such was the power of his name that he was able to rule for twenty years, until Germany revenged herself on France for what the first Napoleon had done.

In a great building in the heart of Paris is the tomb of Napoleon I, draped with flags. But today Frenchmen are beginning to escape from the spell of the legend. They are beginning to see Napoleon for what he was—a great adventurer who spilled the life-blood of millions of men to satisfy his own ambition.

Bolivar

Bolivar Fights for Freedom

ON December 2, 1804, Napoleon Bonaparte knelt in the Cathedral of Notre Dame, in Paris, and taking the crown of France from the hands of the Pope, placed it on his own head, and proclaimed himself Napoleon I, Emperor of the French.

Among the great multitude who stood in the Cathedral and watched the magnificent ceremony was a slender, dark youth, with a lively and expressive face. He was dressed in the latest fashion, and wore a handsome sword; and he carried himself with an air of easy and natural elegance that stamped him as an aristocrat. His eyes, extraordinary for their size and intensity, never for an instant left the little figure of the newly crowned Emperor. And his thoughts ran to this effect:

"Napoleon is the greatest man in the world. No man of our time has ever had so much glory. How wonderful it must be to be praised and acclaimed by an entire nation! Of course, he probably should not have destroyed the republic. But France is still freer than most countries."

Then a shadow crossed his face. "France is free. Yes, but my poor country is still in chains. If only a great man could arise to break those chains—to free South America from the clutch of Spain! What glory that would be!"

Suddenly he found himself thrilling to a new resolve. He would be that man! Somehow—he did not yet know how—he would lead the South Americans in revolt against their harsh Spanish masters.

THE REVOLUTION BREWS

At one time or another, almost every young man says to himself, "I will be famous!" Usually, of course, this is just a dream. But to Simón Bolívar it was more than a dream. He felt greatness within him. He knew that he was a natural leader of men. He had enormous energy. He had a personality that made people listen to him with admiration. He had a keen, quick, and penetrating mind. He wrote well. He talked many languages. He was an aristocrat by birth and education. He was wealthy. He was a friend of kings and statesmen in several countries. If ever there was a man fitted for a great career, it was he.

And his feeling of hatred against Spain was genuine. He himself was a pure-blooded descendant of the Spanish conquerors, and his family owned rich lands and thousands of Indian and Negro slaves in Venezuela, and got along very well under Spanish rule. But he knew that the less fortunate people of South America were miserable, and were becoming more miserable all the time.

South America was governed by Spanish aristocrats, whose job it was to keep order and collect taxes. Most of these taxes they sent to the King of Spain, but they managed to hold on to a good deal for themselves. When one Spanish governor had made his fortune, he would go back to Spain and live the rest of his life in luxury, while another would take his place.

So greedy were these Spaniards for money that they made the

poorest Indians and Negroes pay them a large part of whatever little money they earned, so that many of them died of starvation. And of course, the whites had to pay heavily, too. Those who protested were thrown into horrible dungeons. Sometimes, to frighten the people, the governor would order his soldiers to whip some "rebel" to death, or to fasten him to their horses, and drag him along stony ground for miles, until he died.

Even the Creoles (as the South American aristocrats were called), who were well-to-do and had nothing to worry about, did not like this cruelty. Furthermore, they did not see why all the best government positions and salaries should go to Spaniards. Some of them would have liked to share in the graft.

To make matters worse, the Spanish nobles had a way of turning up their noses at South American customs, and of calling the Creoles "Indians." Since the Creoles, like Bolívar, were very proud of their pure Spanish blood, they deeply resented the way they were treated by visiting grandees from Madrid. Many of the Creoles were ready for a change of government.

Furthermore, almost all the South American merchants and traders, whites and half-breeds, were unhappy under Spanish rule. The Spanish King had turned all trade in South America into a monopoly. The business men there could trade only with Spain, and were allowed to make very little profit. Some of them tried to smuggle in goods from the United States, or from England, or Holland, but when they were caught they were punished or even killed.

THE VOW

You can see, therefore, that there were plenty of reasons for a revolution; and why a sensitive young man like Bolívar was will-

ing to lead one. But it was a risky business. Not only would he be
risking his life—all his wealth and property would, of course, be
seized by the government at the first sign of rebellion.

In later years Bolívar's love of glory, and of being the unquestioned leader, like Napoleon, led him to do things which a man
like George Washington, for example, would never have done.
But this did not prevent him from being just as sincere as Washington in wanting to free his people from foreign tyranny.

As a matter of fact, Bolívar had disliked the Spaniards from
childhood. As a boy he had a tutor, named Rodríguez, who was
an ardent Venezuelan patriot, and had taught his pupil to love
the idea of liberty. Finally the Spanish authorities heard about
his ideas, and Rodríguez was forced to flee to Europe.

When, after Napoleon's coronation, Bolívar left the Cathedral
of Notre Dame, surrounded by his elegant friends, his heart
turned to his old tutor. He felt disgusted with the fashionable,
meaningless life he was leading—tired of women who made a
fuss over him, and of men who talked endlessly about "freedom"
and "liberty" without ever doing anything about it. He would
act! At once! To begin with, he would find Rodríguez.

After a search he heard that Rodríguez was in Italy, in Rome;
and he joined him there. One day the two of them climbed a hill
overlooking the glorious old city, where Rodríguez talked ex-
citingly of the great Roman republic of the past, and of the beauty
of freedom. Carried away, his eyes moist and his face flushed,
Bolívar made a solemn vow: "I swear by the God of my fathers
that I shall not rest until I have freed my native land."

THE FIRST BLOW IS STRUCK

Bolívar went back to Venezuela, to his estates, to wait for an opportunity. Several years passed uneventfully. Meanwhile, he studied military strategy—like Cromwell. Then, in 1810, the opportunity came; and it was Napoleon who made it. For the French Emperor sent an army to Madrid, and deposed the Spanish king, setting up a puppet-king of his own.

When the news came to Caracas, the capital of Venezuela, there was tremendous excitement. With Spain torn, was not this a good time to strike for liberty? A group of Creole aristocrats suddenly seized the palace of the government. They declared that they were for the "rightful" King, and made the governor abdicate. The governor's soldiers did not interfere, because for some time, owing to troubles in Spain, they had not been paid, and they were mutinous.

The rebels knew that shortly new Spanish troops would be coming to attack them, and that they had better raise an army at once. In particular, they needed a general, because most of the good ones were on the Spanish side. Now it happened that a famous Venezuelan general and lover of freedom, named Francisco Miranda, was at that time in London, where he had been trying to raise money for a revolution. The rebel leaders wanted someone to bring Miranda back home in a hurry. They asked Bolívar if he would go, and he consented.

When Miranda and Bolívar returned from England, the general took command of the Venezuelan army, and appointed the young man to command a fortified town named Puerto Cabello. But Bolívar was very discontented with this post. He did not

consider it important enough for him. Besides, the revolution
was not going at all as he liked. The new Spanish forces now
had arrived, and were trying to force a battle. Miranda knew
that his army was weak, and was avoiding a serious fight by re-
treating.

BOLÍVAR BETRAYS HIS CHIEF

Then Bolívar did something which certainly does not seem
like the action of a noble person.

First, without permission, he left his fortress, and it was soon
captured by the Spanish, his soldiers with it. Then he and some
of his fellow-officers joined in a conspiracy against Miranda. They
seized the general and delivered him up to the Spanish commander. True, they urged the Spaniards only to banish Miranda;
but instead the unfortunate man was thrown into prison, where
he died. Bolívar and his friends, however, were treated more
gently, for they were merely exiled to a nearby island; while the
revolutionary army broke up.

Against Bolívar's later achievements this deed stands out like
a splotch of ink on a white wall. Of course, we cannot know
exactly what his reasons were. Possibly he felt that the revolution
would have a better chance later if a truce was made. But it is
also possible that he was acting to save himself, or because he was
jealous of Miranda. We must face the fact that many men whom
we admire do things at one time or another which are unworthy
of them, and even shameful.

SUCCESS?

Bolívar did not stay long in exile. Other countries of South America had also begun to revolt against Spain. West of Venezuela lay the country which is now called Colombia. There the rebels were defeating the Spaniards, and had declared their complete independence from Spain. Bolívar went to Colombia, and joined the army as an officer. He helped to drive out some remaining Spanish troops, and revealed true bravery and skill. Then he asked the Colombian Congress to give him troops to lead against the Spaniards in Venezuela; because, he told them, neither country would be safe from Spain until both were free. They agreed, and in appreciation of his services made him a general and gave him a little army of 800 men.

Then began a remarkable campaign. Bolívar led his small band into Venezuela, and began to rally the people to his flag. He threatened the Spaniards, and those who were loyal to Spain, with "war to the death." Later on this phrase would come back to trouble him. But now his army grew, and the hopes of the country grew with it. In three months Bolívar marched 700 miles, won six pitched battles, and captured the capital, Caracas.

When he entered the city, most of the people were overjoyed. Twelve beautiful girls, so it is said, came out to greet him with a triumphal carriage. Then they pulled the carriage through the streets themselves, while he stood erect, bowing to the cheering crowds, who hailed him as their "Liberator." Bolívar always liked festivals and parades in his honor. But since Latin American people love to hold celebrations, they did not consider this a weakness on his part; on the contrary, it endeared him to them.

Proclaiming Venezuela a republic, Bolívar called a Congress together and drew up a constitution. The Congress gave him the title of "Liberator," and he said, "I deem this title a greater honor than the scepters of all the empires in the world!" It seemed to many that he had succeeded—that Venezuela was free.

THE LLANEROS

But a great danger was forming against him. On the grassy plains of Venezuela, where cattle were raised, were many thousands of Indians and half-breeds known as *llaneros*. They were really the cowboys of the country—wild, fierce men, natural-born fighters, the best in Venezuela. Bolívar thought that they would join the revolution, because they had been badly treated by the Spaniards. But the Spaniards had sent a man named José Boves to win the *llaneros* over to their side.

Boves was a hulking brute of a man, as tough as they come—a pirate, smuggler, and robber. Bolívar once said of him, "He was not nourished with milk, but with the blood of tigers." Boves gave the *llaneros* money, and promised that if they followed him he would let them rob and loot to their hearts' content. He told them too that the blue-blooded Bolívar had threatened them with "war to the death." "Well," he said, "let us give him what he wants." The *llaneros* sharpened their machetes—the deadly knives which they use—and grinned.

Bolívar, meanwhile, was having trouble in running the new government. He was not a great ruler, of the Richelieu type. Food was scarce, and prices were high, and there was not much money. People began to complain. Then Boves and his army began to ride through the country, burning and killing and robbing. Soon the people were saying that Bolívar's threat of "war to the death" was responsible for the cruelty of the *llaneros;* and the complaints became louder still.

For a year Bolívar managed to defend the larger cities of Venezuela against Boves. Once, angered by the savage ways of the *llaneros,* he ordered his men to shoot 886 Spanish prisoners of war—an act for which he has been sharply blamed, and which certainly was not in accordance with his high principles. But we must remember that in wartime men's passions become inflamed, and they are likely to do things on impulse which they would never do in cold blood.

It became harder and harder for Bolívar to raise the money and troops he needed. Boves continued to attack and, at last, in June 1814 he smashed Bolívar's army in a bloody battle, and captured Caracas once more for the Spaniards.

FAILURE?

By this time, not only the people but even his own army officers were bitter against Bolívar. There was a violent quarrel between him and his staff, who blamed him for the defeat of the army; and he left Venezuela in disgrace.

He went at once to Colombia, where he explained to the Congress why he had lost; because of the "blindness of the native Venezuelans," who had not supported his fight for independence. But he said that he was still confident of the future.

The Congress of Colombia said to him, "As a military commander you have been unfortunate, but you are a great man." Again they put him in charge of some troops. He was told to march against the last Spanish fortress in Colombia. But now, unfortunately, his pride and ambition got him into trouble again. He and one of the Colombian generals began to quarrel over who was to be commander-in-chief. This delayed Bolívar's attack on the Spaniards so long that they were able to bring up reinforcements. By the time he finally went into action against them, they were strong enough to defeat his army, inflicting serious losses.

The Colombian Congress and the people were indignant at Bolívar, and refused to give him another army to lead. So there was nothing to do but resign and leave the country. He wrote "a proclamation," in which he tried to justify himself, but nobody paid any attention. Then he sailed for Jamaica.

This was the low point of his career. Both in Venezuela and in Colombia people had washed their hands of him. In Jamaica, a man tried to stab him. The British decided that they did not want him in their territory, so he had to leave Jamaica.

He went to Haiti, where the Negro President received him with honor. In return, Bolívar promised to free all the slaves in Venezuela—some day.

"THE ART OF VICTORY IS TO BE LEARNED IN DEFEAT"

But even now Bolívar was not disheartened. He was one of those men who never admit defeat. You might crush him; but like a rubber ball, when the pressure was released, he would spring back into shape again. He himself said, "The art of victory is to be learned in defeat."

The Spaniards, having conquered Venezuela, sent a strong army to Colombia and occupied that country also. The other revolutionary leaders fled, or were killed. Again the backbone of the revolution seemed to be broken. But Bolívar decided that the time had come to try again. He raised a little band of 250 men, most of them foreign adventurers, American, Irish, English, and French, and with this "army" sailed for Venezuela.

His first act on landing was to keep his promise to the President of Haiti and issue a dramatic proclamation freeing the slaves. (This, remember, was in 1815, almost fifty years before the slaves in the United States were freed by Lincoln.) An early defeat forced him to go back to Haiti for more recruits and guns, but presently he was in action again. Then, to his delight, he was able to win the *llaneros* over to his side, for Boves had died, and their new leader, Páez, was friendly to the revolution.

VICTORY AT LAST

True, a strong Spanish army defeated the *llaneros* in a battle in which Bolívar was wounded. His spirit, however, remained strong. In another proclamation he spoke of "a free and united South America," and he wrote to the revolutionaries in far-off Argentina, encouraging them.

By 1819, his "foreign legion" had grown considerably, for all over the world adventurous men and lovers of freedom had heard of his great fight, and had gone to join his ranks. Particularly he was aided by an Englishman named Rooke, an Irishman named O'Leary, and a Jew named Bríon. Together with the remnants of the *llaneros,* Bolívar could muster about 2500 experienced fighting troops.

Suddenly he determined on a move of amazing boldness, which was to prove decisive. Leaving Venezuela, he marched his army across the freezing Andes mountains into Colombia— one of the greatest military feats in history. Then, while his men were still weary and hungry, he smashed a Spanish army twice the size of his. Finally, against desperate odds, he drove the Spaniards out of Colombia altogether.

He was becoming more and more brilliant as a general. It is doubtful whether even a Napoleon could have done better than Bolívar did in this campaign. And although he too insisted on absolute obedience from his men, he was never as harsh a commander as Napoleon. Once, preparing to attack a Spanish stronghold, he gave the order to one of his officers: "Attack before lunch." The officer misunderstood, and told his men to eat their lunch before attacking. While they were at it, Bolívar rode up in a howling rage at the delay.

"You are no longer in command!" he shouted.

The officer was a gallant soldier, and he also understood Bolívar's character. He did not argue. Instead he threw away his sword, and seized a musket. "General," he said, "if I am not fit to lead this attack as commander, let me take part in it as a private."

That was exactly the kind of dramatic gesture that Bolívar loved. He threw his arms around the officer, and cried, "You are reinstated! Lead the attack!"

These outbursts of generous feeling endeared him to his troops as time went on, and helped to bring him new recruits. Finally he was able to leave Colombia, and march back to Venezuela. This was the beginning of a grand success. With Colombia behind him, hailing him as its own Liberator, with the Spaniards of Venezuela suffering from lack of reinforcements, it was only a matter of time before Bolívar was able to free Venezuela too. In 1822, he proclaimed the Republic of Greater Colombia, which included the present countries of Venezuela, Colombia, and

Ecuador; and a Congress named him President and "Supreme Chief."

AMBITION AGAIN

Now all through South America the revolution triumphed—in Panama to the north and Argentina and Chile to the south. Only Peru still remained in Spanish hands, for Brazil was Portuguese territory.

The Liberator of Argentina and Chile was a man named José de San Martín. He was less brilliant than Bolívar, but everyone respected him for his sincerity and courage. San Martín led an army into Peru, and set up a temporary government with himself as Protector, until such time as the Spanish forces could be finally beaten, and a Congress could be assembled.

Bolívar did not agree with San Martín's ideas, and he was not pleased to see another man get the credit for liberating Peru. So he too sent an army there, and invited San Martín to talk things over. San Martín accepted eagerly, for he admired Bolívar as a great hero. The two of them had a long, secret conference.

Then a strange thing happened. San Martín left the conference room heavy-hearted and sad, a changed man. He immediately resigned his post as Protector of Peru, and sailed back to Argentina. After that, he never again took an active part in politics. To his friends he said nothing about Bolívar—except when one bitter little phrase escaped his lips: "He is not the man we thought him."

What had taken place? It seems that the two men did not agree on the kind of government Peru should have. Bolívar was the more persuasive talker. He told San Martín that the country would be better off under the kind of republic he wanted to set up; and San Martín, although not convinced, did not want to create a split in the revolutionary forces. Some say, furthermore, that the idealistic San Martín realized that Bolívar was ambitious for personal glory at any cost. After that he was so disappointed in his hero that in disgust he determined to give up politics entirely.

However that may be, Bolívar quickly led the Peruvian rebels to victory, and was proclaimed Liberator of Peru. Then he freed the country now called Bolivia in his honor. At this point you can see the finer side of his character. In gratitude, the Peruvian Congress offered him a million dollars as a gift. But although he had lost all his property and money, Bolívar refused. He loved glory, but he had an aristocratic contempt for money-grubbers.

THE POLITICIANS AND THE PEOPLE

Spain had been driven out of South America, once and for all. Bolívar was President of Greater Colombia. But now he had to face a new crop of troubles.

The chief of these troubles lay in the fact that most of the people of his country, and of most of the rest of South America, were not a great deal better off under the republic than they had been under Spain.

The people who benefited most from the revolution were the professional politicians, and the large landholders, and wealthy families. These men now got the best government jobs and salaries and graft—for they did not worry much about being honest. They got themselves elected to Congress, and saw to it that the taxes of the new government came mostly from the poorer classes, because they themselves wanted to pay as little as possible.

You may ask, why did the people elect these politicians to Congress? The answer is that they did not know any better. Most of the people were Indians and half-breeds, and poor whites who did not even know how to read and write. They believed what they were told. If they voted at all, they voted the way their bosses wanted them to vote. Even today in the United States a great many people vote in just that way. It is not surprising that conditions were so undemocratic in the new South American republics a century ago.

Furthermore, once the Spanish trade monopoly was broken, a great many foreign business men swooped down on the new countries like hawks. They bribed or persuaded the politicians to buy their goods for the government at high prices, and to sell them the crops of the Indians and the Negroes at low prices. This, of course, left the masses of the people almost as poor as they had been under Spain.

"PLOWING IN THE SEA"

Soon the foreign merchants and the aristocrats and the politicians were growing rich, while the rest of the people were miserable. But they did not know whom to blame for their misery. They did not know how to get the laws passed that would give them more land, or reduce taxes and prices. All they knew was that they could hardly get enough to eat, and could not afford decent houses, or clothing, or medicines.

Bolívar saw all this. And he was truly sorry about it. But he did not know what to do, either. He was afraid to anger the foreign merchants, especially the English ones, because he wanted to borrow money from England. To get it, he had to let the English business men make a big profit at the expense of his country.

And he was afraid to insist on democratic laws that might have helped the poor, because that would have angered the wealthy classes, and stirred up new rebellions. Besides, he saw that the people did not know enough to govern themselves.

You may say, why didn't he build schools and educate the people in democratic government? At one time he started to, but he never got far; for he did not dare arouse the wrath of the Catholic Church, which had control of education, and which did not approve of democratic government.

The total result of Bolívar's revolution, as you can see, was to transfer control of the country from a small group of selfish Spaniards to a small group of selfish Creoles and foreign business men, together with a few Indians and half-breeds who were clever enough to be politicians.

Bolívar could only sigh and bemoan the fate of his people. He saw that for a long while to come they would be robbed and squeezed by unscrupulous politicians and business men and landowners; and he said bitterly, "I have been plowing in the sea"— meaning that all his work had been for nothing.

Revolutions, as you can see, may be a good thing for the revolutionary leaders, who seize power and get money and glory. And they may be a good thing for the people too—but only if the revolutionary leaders are sincere enough and strong enough to pass laws which give poor people higher wages, and which lower the prices of bread and clothing, and the rent of houses and land. Unless these things are done and schools are built, most of the

people do not get enough out of the revolution to justify the suffering and hardship of the struggle.

"I FEAR PEACE MORE THAN WAR"

Bolívar shook his head, saying that he feared peace more than
war—for he saw that the problems of peace were harder to solve.
Because the people were unhappy, they were willing to listen to
anyone who promised to help them. And of course, there were a
number of politicians who were perfectly willing to make such
promises in order to gain more power. Among these were some
of Bolívar's former army officers, whom he had made governors
in various provinces. They were jealous of Bolívar, and ambitious; so they said to the people, "Let us revolt against Greater
Colombia. Once we are independent, we will be better off."

The people did not realize that this so-called "independence"
alone could not help them. They needed rulers who really cared
about them, and better laws. A new revolution would only transfer power from one hard-fisted crowd to another. But the word
"independence" has a fine sound, so they followed the new rebel
leaders, and began to demand separate countries.

Bolívar knew that new changes in government would not help
the people, and that having a lot of little countries would only
cause wars to start. But he wanted to avoid bloodshed. So when
his former lieutenant, the *llanero* chieftain Páez, demanded that
Venezuela be made practically independent, he reluctantly gave
in. This encouraged rebels in Ecuador to start trouble. Then in
Colombia itself a "popular" party began to demand that Bolívar
resign; and since this party had obtained control of Congress,
Bolívar had to give up his office.

THE LIBERATOR TURNS DICTATOR

He was tired and ill at the time, and said that he was through with politics. But he was wrong. He would never be through with politics until he died.

The popular party in the Colombia Congress was led by a certain General Santander, who now became President in Bolívar's place. He was an able and sincere man, who had fought bravely in the revolutionary wars. He thought Bolívar's type of government favored the wealthy classes—as it did—and was unfair to the people.

Many of the big landowners and foreign business men and bishops of the Church were afraid of Santander, whom they considered a "radical." Soon this group begged Bolívar to return to the capital, Bogotá, and resume command of the government. They wanted him to drive out Santander and the Congress, and set up a dictatorship, keeping the old laws which they liked.

Bolívar was doubtful. Was he, the Great Liberator, now to become a dictator? But his love for glory and power was as strong as ever, and he had never forgotten his admiration for Napoleon. Besides, he disapproved of Santander's government as much as Santander disapproved of his. At last he consented. His wealthy backers provided an army for him, and in June 1828 he led his troops into Bogotá. The people hailed him, as usual, for his name still had magic; Santander was forced to give up his power; and Congress was dismissed.

In this way, Bolívar challenged the republic which he himself had made. But his conscience troubled him. He felt that he had done the wrong thing. Addressing the people, he said wearily, "I shall not talk to you of liberty. . . . Who can talk of liberty under a dictatorship? Let us pity the people who obey and the man who rules alone."

REBELLION

But he was a gentle dictator. He did not try to imprison or kill his opponents, or build up a spy system. As a result, some of his opponents were able to plot against his life. One night they came in a crowd to the President's palace, shouting, "Death to the tyrant!" But the warning of a woman who loved him gave Bolívar a chance to leave the palace by a side door, and hide underneath a bridge nearby. He had to spend the whole night there. Meanwhile several of his guards were killed in the palace.

In the morning, however, Bolívar's troops rescued him and captured the conspirators. The leaders of the plot were condemned to death, and Bolívar's friends demanded that he order Santander himself to be shot. For although Santander had not been an active conspirator, they knew that he would always be dangerous to the dictatorship. However, Bolívar gallantly refused to kill his rival. Instead, he banished Santander from the country.

As the months went by, Bolívar found it harder and harder to keep order in the distressed country. He no longer cared much about liberty. Once he said bitterly, "Bayonets are the best, the only rulers of nations." Although still a young man, as rulers go, he was tired, and his idealism was gone. Futhermore, his lungs had become affected by tuberculosis, and his energies were failing. At last, revolutions against his dictatorship broke out in a number of places at the same time. He saw that he could no longer govern the country, so he resigned.

His friends were panic-stricken, and made plans to bring a
European prince to Colombia, and set up a monarchy to preserve
their property and wealth. But this was too much for Bolívar,
who still hated kings, even though he did not think much of
democracy. He told his friends to cease their efforts, and to call
a new Congress. Meanwhile, he appointed his best friend and
favorite aide, a general named Sucre, to take his place.

"YOU ARE MORE FORTUNATE THAN I"

Bolívar thought that his health might improve if he went to
Europe, so he started for the coast to find a ship. Now that he was
no longer dictator, the people's love for him returned. They
lined the streets of the towns through which he passed, and
cheered him, and wept for him. The British minister to Colombia
said what was in everybody's heart: "He is gone—the great gentleman of Colombia." And his friend Sucre wrote him, "Good-
by, my general. Receive as a token of my friendship the tears I
am shedding at this moment. Be happy, wherever you are going."

Bolívar had never thought about money, and he was now so
poor that he could not pay for his passage to Europe. While he
was at the seaport, wondering what to do, came terrible news—
Sucre had been murdered in Bogotá. Bolívar was stricken with
grief. Then messengers arrived from his frightened political
friends, urging him to return. But he was too tired and ill. He
wrote to his friends, "I am about to die. My life is finished. God
calls me. . . . I see no salvation for my country. . . . Since I am
unable to secure the happiness of my country, I refuse to rule it.
. . . I no longer have any country for which to make sacrifices."

Instead of going back to Bogotá, he retired to a little house in the mountains, where he became more and more feeble. One of his last conversations was with his doctor, a Frenchman who had come to Colombia.

"What did you seek in this country, Doctor?"

"Liberty, your Excellency," the doctor answered.

"And have you found it?"

"Yes, your Excellency."

"Then," said Bolívar with a faint smile, "you are more fortunate than I."

A few days later the great man died. He was forty-seven years old—almost the same age as Napoleon, when he was sent to St. Helena.

GLORY AT LAST

Bolívar's life was a tragedy—far more tragic than Napoleon's. Yet after his death he won the glory for which he had yearned all his life. Today, in the great continent to the south, his name above all others is spoken with admiration and respect. From Venezuela to Argentina, from Brazil to Peru, the peoples of South America revere the memory of Simón Bolívar. They speak of him as The Great Liberator; and in every city streets and public buildings bear his name or statue.

Yet it cannot be said that the "liberty" which Bolívar gave to his people solved their problems. For although it was liberty from Spain, it was not liberty from native politicians, or from greedy foreign business men, or from tight-fisted plantation owners, or from the ignorance of the people themselves. Possibly there was no way in which he could have helped them to get rid of these forces of tyranny.

Before he died, he had learned a sad truth. Having a republic does not in itself give freedom to a people. They must learn how to use their right to vote intelligently. They must learn how to prevent greedy, selfish politicians from taking power and fooling them with false promises. They must learn how to distinguish between a law which will help them, and a law which can only hurt them; between an honest, able man, and a crooked or weak man. They must raise their voices loudly in protest against men who seek to get rich at their expense. Only in that way can they prevent tyrants from taking advantage of them, in a republic as well as in a kingdom.

SOUTH AMERICA AND THE FUTURE

In the century since Bolívar's death, many tyrants have come and gone in all the South American countries. There have been revolutions by the hundreds, bloody wars between the nations, dictatorships, cruel years of terror. But little by little the people have begun to learn more about government. They have gradually taken away some of the power of the foreign business men, and are helping their own businesses. They stand proudly on their own feet, and will not let any foreign nation, not even the United States, tell them what to do. They have become more and more unwilling to allow politicians to set up dictatorships and steal from the public treasury.

Today the South American countries are learning to respect the rights of the Indians and Negroes, and poor people generally. Working men have begun to demand decent wages. And slowly —very slowly—the people are learning the meaning of democracy.

There can be no doubt that South America will in the future

grow more and more prosperous as the masses of the people become less ignorant and begin to develop their great resources.
North Americans already realize this fact, and their eyes are
turning south. It is quite possible that before long South America will be the new "land of opportunity," and that great numbers of dissatisfied Europeans and Americans will go there to
seek their fortunes and make their homes, as many have already
done.

At the root of real prosperity and real democracy is the education of the masses of the people. Bolívar could not do much in
this respect; or possibly he did not understand how to go about
it. He put too much reliance on the word "liberty," and gave too
little attention to the real facts of food, clothing, houses, schools,
and honest newspapers. Still, he did not live in vain. For his
dramatic career was in a sense the starting point of the modern
history of South America, which seems to be moving toward a
future better than the past.

Bismarck

Bismarck Builds an Empire

I N German universities, students of aristocratic birth are accustomed to make a sport out of dueling. Even today they cover up their bodies with thick padding and slash away at each other's faces with sharp swords; and they do not stop until one is badly wounded. Sometimes students have been killed when a sword has accidentally pierced a vital spot. But they consider it a matter of honor to take part in these duels, and are very proud of their scars.

In the year 1833, a young university student named Otto von Bismarck had a great reputation as a duelist. In a single summer he took part in thirty-two duels, and won almost all of them. For he was a strong, fierce fighter, who would never even wince when he was wounded, and who never lost his head when he was being attacked.

As a student, young Bismarck gave no hint of future greatness. He seldom attended lectures, and he spent a great deal of his time in wild drinking bouts with other aristocratic students, and in riding through the countryside, for he was a splendid horseman. Nevertheless, he managed to pass his examinations and to become a lawyer.

Although no man with so much spirit and love of action could like being cooped up in an office, when he graduated from the university, his family, who were Junkers—aristocratic Prussian landowners—insisted that he become a government official. He started work in a government bureau. After a few months, however, he could no longer stand having to obey orders and write reports. When his father became ill, he gladly gave up his job, and went home to manage the family estates, where he could ride and drink and carouse to his heart's content.

In spite of his reputation for recklessness, he was wise enough to develop his mind. He read a great deal of German and foreign literature, learned several languages, and traveled to England and France. Gradually, too, he became interested in religion and politics, which he used to discuss with the other Junkers in his neighborhood. Finally Bismarck fell in love with the daughter of one of these neighbors, and gave up his wild ways in order to marry her.

BISMARCK ATTRACTS ATTENTION

From his childhood on, Bismarck was a Prussian patriot, who wanted to see Prussia become the mightiest nation in Europe. For after the fall of Napoleon I, Prussia had gradually regained her power, and Prussians were again proud of their fatherland.

There were two strong political parties in Prussia. One was the Conservative party, to which Bismarck belonged. The Conservatives were against changes. They believed that the King of Prussia and his ministers should go right on making laws as they wished, as in the days of Frederick the Great, and that it was the duty of the people to obey without question. The other party was the Liberals, who thought that the business men and landowners should have a parliament, as in England, so that they could have something to say about laws.

In those days railroads were being built and new machines were being invented all over Europe, and business was becoming more and more important. Finally, in the year 1847 the Liberals insisted that the King call a parliament together, and he thought it best to consent. Although there had been parliaments in England and France for centuries, this was the first parliament in Prussian history; and it really did not amount to much, because the King gave it no rights except the right to talk.

Bismarck was not elected to this would-be parliament. But a member who was a friend of his became ill, and could not go; and Bismarck was sent in his place.

At first nobody in the parliament paid much attention to this big, brawny young man with the strong face and fierce eyes. For a while he sat quietly listening to the arguments. Then one day he got to his feet and spoke. He was not a great speaker, for he hesitated, and sought for words. But what he said made the Liberals furious. He wanted to abolish the parliament and to see Prussia once more a state without political parties, "united under our beloved ruler."

This, if you remember, was very much like the speech with which Richelieu won the favor of Queen Marie. And it worked out in about the same way for Bismarck. The ruler of Prussia, Frederick William IV, and his ministers were delighted with this bold defense of the "divine right" of kings. They invited Bismarck to the palace, and talked with him, and were deeply impressed by his powerful personality.

THE YEAR OF REVOLUTION

The parliament broke up without having accomplished anything, and Bismarck went back home. A few months later, early
in the year 1848, there was another revolution in France. The
French King was overthrown, and a republic was set up. Similar
trouble then broke out in Austria and the German states. In Berlin crowds marched in the street demanding that the King abdicate.

The reason for these uprisings was that the business men of
Europe were indignant at the kings and aristocrats. They wanted
more freedom to buy and sell, and make profits without interference. And they were supported by a great many miserable
workmen who were receiving very small wages, and who lived
for the most part in horrible slums or dingy huts in the country.
These unfortunate people thought that a parliament would help
them.

When Bismarck saw what was happening he rushed to Berlin
and talked with King Frederick William. His idea was that the
King should call out his troops and shoot down the unruly citizens. He believed in "the iron hand." But the King feared a civil
war. He decided that he would allow the people to have a parliament, and give business men something to say about the laws. A
constitution to this effect was drawn up, and this pacified the
Liberals and restored order.

At first Bismarck refused to be a member of the new parliament. He began to write articles for the Berlin newspapers, violently demanding that full power be given back to the King.

Naturally, the business men and the laborers soon regarded him as their worst enemy, and hated him.

Presently, seeing that the parliament was going to remain, he got himself elected to it, and made more enemies by his bitter attacks on the Liberals. He detested Liberals almost as much as Adolf Hitler does today. Once a friend and neighbor of Bismarck's remarked that he had joined the Liberal party, and was going to make some speeches against the monarchy. Bismarck was enraged by what he regarded as "treason" by a Junker to his class. Grimly he told his friend, "If you do that, I shall shoot you."

His friend was taken aback at the seriousness of Bismarck's manner. "You would not do that," he said.

"I give you my word of honor that I would," said Bismarck. "You know that I am a man of my word. Believe me, you had better not make those speeches."

And the friend obeyed.

BISMARCK DREAMS OF A PRUSSIAN EMPIRE

All his life Bismarck had two ideas about government. The first was that the King of Prussia should be absolute. The second was that the German states should be united into a great empire under Prussian leadership.

In those days, most of the wealthy people of Prussia and Saxony and Bavaria and Hanover and the numerous other little German states were envious of France and Austria and Russia, which were large, strong countries. They wanted Germany to be powerful, too, for then she could make other countries do more business with her, and Germans would make more money. There was much talk of "a united German empire."

It was easier to say "let us unite" than to do it. In the first place, the kings and princes and dukes who ruled in independent German states were not anxious to give up their thrones. Then again, they could not agree who ought to be emperor. Some said the Emperor of Austria should be the Emperor of Germany too. Others preferred the King of Prussia.

Finally they sent their statesmen to try to work out a plan. This conference met in the German city of Frankfurt, and after a long discussion decided to ask the Prussian King to become emperor. Their idea was to give him only a little power, and to have an elected parliament make the important laws.

When King Frederick William received this invitation, he was tempted. For one thing, he was afraid that if he did not accept, the Austrian Emperor would. Some of his ministers advised him to accept. Then he consulted Bismarck.

In his forceful way, Bismarck said, "I beg Your Majesty to refuse!" "Why?" demanded the King. Bismarck explained. To accept the crown without the power meant nothing. It would be giving in to the Liberals. The imperial crown of Germany, said Bismarck, must come to Prussia because of Prussia's might! "The Prussian eagle," Bismarck proclaimed, "will only be able to spread its wings over all Germany if it has free use of them!"

The King was impressed, and wrote the Frankfurt conference that he would not accept the crown on their terms—he would not lower himself to become "the serf of the revolution." Then he sent Bismarck to Frankfurt to make sure that the crown was not offered to Austria. This was Bismarck's first important political assignment.

ONWARD TO FAME

War with Austria was in the air. The question had to be decided: was Austria or Prussia going to be the most important country in central Europe? In 1850 many Prussians thought that their King should declare war on Austria. To the general surprise, Bismarck made a powerful speech against war. He said that to fight Austria at that time would be costly and dangerous. It would strengthen the Liberal party. It would mean trouble at home.

"Wait," he advised the King privately. "Wait until our army is stronger." Again the King followed his advice.

Soon a new crisis arose. Napoleon III had seized the throne of France, and he and the English were sending troops to fight Russia, in the region known as Crimea. Frederick William disliked Napoleon, and thought of helping the Russian Czar. Bismarck advised him not to. "In politics," he said, "no man does anything for his neighbor unless it is to his own interest."

As Bismarck had counseled, Prussia stayed out of the war. Now the King's other ministers began to be envious of Bismarck's growing importance. Frederick William was old, and was losing his mind, and these jealous statesmen tried to turn him against Bismarck. Finally they persuaded him to send Bismarck away from Prussia, to become ambassador to Russia. Bismarck did not like the idea at all. He said, "I have been sent into exile!" But he nevertheless went to St. Petersburg (now Leningrad).

As things turned out, he was an excellent ambassador. The Czar of Russia liked hunting, and Bismarck was an excellent shot with a gun, as well as a superb horseman. These qualities, together with his strong personality and high intelligence, quickly won him the friendship of the Russian royal family—a friendship which was later useful to Prussia and Bismarck.

Two years later Frederick William died, an insane old man, and since he had no sons, his brother, William, became king. William knew Bismarck, and approved of his ideas. He called him back to Berlin and offered to make him one of the ministers of the Crown. Bismarck, however, was not willing to be just a member of the ministry. He wanted to be prime minister.

Declining the king's offer with thanks, he asked instead to be sent as ambassador to Paris, to study Napoleon III and conditions in France. King William consented, and to Paris Bismarck went. He was then forty-six years old.

BISMARCK CRUSHES PARLIAMENT

The King's troubles with parliament were—of course—mainly over the question of taxes. King William was a soldier by training, and he wanted a powerful army. This meant more taxes, and parliament refused to grant them, unless it could control part of the troops.

Like Charles I under similar circumstances, William was indignant. His commander-in-chief, General von Moltke, urged him to stand firm and to dissolve the parliament. But the King was afraid of a revolution, and hesitated. None of his ministers was strong enough to help him. Finally he realized that there was only one man who might be able to handle parliament—Bismarck. Hastily he sent a message to Paris, asking his ambassador to become prime minister.

Bismarck hurried back to Berlin, and at once entered the hall of parliament and faced the members. They shouted questions at him. What was the reason for increasing the army? Why were these new taxes necessary? Was there going to be a war?

Bismarck smiled contemptuously. He knew that Prussia would soon fight Austria, but he certainly did not intend to say so. He refused to answer any questions, and insisted that the new tax laws be passed. The members debated, and got nowhere. Then Bismarck acted. He declared parliament dissolved. The new Prussian constitution, he said, was only "a piece of paper." The people would have to pay the new taxes whether parliament liked it or not.

The public protested. There was talk of revolution. But Bismarck knew how to keep his people quiet. He called for elections to another parliament. So! the Liberals said. He had decided to respect the constitution, after all. Good!

Bismarck, however, was merely fooling the people. When the new parliament, too, refused to approve the tax laws, he quickly dissolved it. Again the public objected, and again he kept them quiet with the same trick. Three times more he summoned parliament, only to send the members home again.

Meanwhile, his tax collectors were demanding money, and the obedient Prussian people were reluctantly paying up. By the time the public awoke to the meaning of all this coming and going of parliaments, it was too late to do much about it. The taxes had been collected, and parliament had lost its power.

Although as a politician Bismarck was harsh and domineering, as a man he had a generous side. Once he found it necessary to order the arrest of a young man who made some unwise political speeches. On the day when he was to give the order, he rose early, and went himself to the young man's lodging. There he climbed three flights of stairs, and routed the bewildered young fellow out of bed. "You had better leave for foreign parts at once," Bismarck said sharply.

When the young man finally realized who was talking to him, he was so amazed that he could barely manage to thank Bismarck. Then it turned out that he could not leave, because he had no money. Bismarck put some on the table and strode out of the room. All his life he had a weak spot for adventurous young men, and gave them a helping hand when he could.

BLOOD AND IRON

Prussia was now once more a dictatorship. And Bismarck was more unpopular than ever. But he did not care. To become dictator in a republic—as Napoleon did—a man must be liked by the masses of the people; but to become dictator in a monarchy— as Bismarck did—a man need only be liked by the King and the aristocrats.

Although the King liked Bismarck, he was also afraid of him. Not long after Bismarck came to power they had a sharp quarrel. The Austrian Emperor and the rulers of the other German states were working again on a plan for a German empire and they invited King William to attend a new conference. William was inclined to go. He thought that Prussia and Austria might settle the question of who was to rule Germany, without war.

Bismarck overwhelmed the King with a storm of arguments. "Nothing," he said, "can solve the question but blood and iron!" Why, he asked the King, should we give way now, when we are so nearly ready?

Ready for what? There was a plan, which had been worked out by Bismarck and General von Moltke. It was such a plan as to appeal to the heart of William, who was himself a soldier. For it was a plan of war. It began in the north, in Denmark; it continued in the south, in Austria; and it ended in the west, in France. The time had come for "blood and iron."

THE FIRST VICTIM: DENMARK

Up north, in little Denmark, there was trouble brewing. Denmark then owned a province called Schleswig-Holstein. A German prince was arguing with the Danish King about who was the rightful ruler of this territory. Suddenly Bismarck stepped in, saying in effect, "It doesn't belong to either of you. Prussia must have Schleswig-Holstein."

The fact that he had no legal claim did not bother him at all, any more than it had bothered Frederick the Great. The Danish King protested, and appealed to France and England. But neither of them would give him any help. Finally little Denmark prepared to defend herself as well as she could.

Bismarck was worried that Austria might interfere at the last moment. He proposed to the Austrian Emperor that they act together. An army of Austrians and Prussians marched north together, won some easy battles, and in three weeks had conquered Schleswig-Holstein. England finally protested, but Bismarck merely grinned, for he knew that the English would not fight over this matter. In our own time, Adolf Hitler seized Czecho-Slovakia in a very similar way.

King William of Prussia was so delighted that he made Bismarck a count. But parliament objected that Bismarck had no right to go to war and make peace without their consent. In reply, Bismarck sneered that parliament had nothing to do with politics—only with debates. Then he added injury to insult by sending the members home and telling them to stay there.

Now he became so unpopular among the common people that the King became worried—especially after an attempt was made to kill Bismarck while he was walking on the street. But he escaped with a slight wound, and went on as before, not caring whether the people liked him or not. In this respect, too, he was much like Cardinal Richelieu.

THE SECOND VICTIM: AUSTRIA

As Bismarck expected, Austria and Prussia soon disagreed over who was to rule Schleswig-Holstein. Bismarck settled the question by simply sending in more troops and seizing the whole province for Prussia. Austria was furious. Soon everybody could see that war was about to begin between the two "allies."

But before Bismarck could allow the Prussian armies to march into Austria, he had to make sure that France, England, Russia, and the German states would not help his enemy, and that the angry Prussian Liberals would not stir up trouble. He handled them all with his usual shrewdness.

The Russian royal family were his friends, so they were easily persuaded. He pointed out to England that she had nothing to gain by helping Austria. He encouraged Napoleon III to think that the war would be evenly matched, and that in time France could act as peace-maker, and gain glory and some German territory. As for the other German states, Bismarck told them that if they dared encourage Austria, he would attack them too; and he actually did send troops into Hanover and Saxony, and dethroned the kings of those countries.

Meanwhile he kept the Liberals quiet by summoning parliament, pretending that he was going to prepare a great "reform plan" to give parliament more power. They were so anxious for this plan that they stopped objecting to his warlike policy. But in his heart he never really intended to let them put the plan into effect.

At last he told General von Moltke to go ahead. The scheme of the war had been figured out long before by Moltke, who was probably the best European general since Napoleon. Three Prussian armies marched into Austria separately, and came together near a town called Königgrätz. There they awaited the Austrians. King William of Prussia, Bismarck, and Moltke traveled to Königgrätz to see the battle—just as some wealthy sportsmen nowadays go a thousand miles to see a championship prizefight.

The Austrians were confident, because they had the larger army. But they did not know that the Prussians had a new kind of rifle, which fired much more quickly than the Austrian guns. These guns slaughtered the unfortunate Austrian troops, until the survivors fled. All over Europe the startling news was flashed that Prussia in a single battle had broken her enemy's strength.

BISMARCK FOOLS NAPOLEON III

Napoleon III and the French were alarmed when they heard what had happened at Königgrätz. Prussia was more powerful than they had thought. Napoleon still believed, however, that Bismarck was afraid of France, and he sent a sharp message to the King of Prussia, saying that France was going to act as peace-maker, and that the war must stop.

Bismarck did not want trouble with France—not yet. On the other hand, he certainly did not intend to withdraw his troops before Austria surrendered. So he sent a very clever reply to Napoleon. He said the Prussians would be delighted to have France suggest the terms of peace, and they would stop fighting as soon as they knew what the terms were. Meanwhile, he told the Prussian troops to keep on going; and he announced his own peace terms.

All the statesmen in Europe laughed at the way Bismarck had tricked the French. Since Napoleon was not ready for war, there was nothing for him to do but agree to Bismarck's terms. As a result, Prussia was able to gobble up a number of neighboring German states with very little objection, and Austria lost all her hopes of leading the future German empire.

BISMARCK BECOMES A POPULAR HERO

The great military triumph over Austria and the diplomatic triumph over France made the Prussian common people change their minds about Bismarck. Almost overnight he became a hero. He was considered the most brilliant statesman in the world. Even the parliament voted to give Bismarck a great sum of money and valuable estates as a reward. He himself was amused by the change in public feeling. "Yes," he laughed once, "now I am a great man. But if we had lost at Königgrätz, I should have been the greatest rascal in Germany."

But as he became popular with the business men and the work-ing people, the aristocrats turned against him. The war with

Austria, although short, had cost a great deal of money, and Bismarck had made the Junkers pay more taxes. They were annoyed, too, over the harsh way in which he had pushed the princes of other German states off their thrones. As aristocrats themselves, the Prussian Junkers believed that all aristocratic titles and privileges ought to be respected.

Bismarck, like Richelieu, did not intend to let aristocrats or anybody else stand in his way. When he saw that the Conservatives were turning against him, he made a deal with the Liberal party. He told them that if they would support him, he would make some laws that would help business. In this way he was able to become the leader of a very strong party in parliament, which passed the laws that he wanted. So long as parliament did what he wished he was perfectly willing to have it take part in government. Then he was able to say that he was only ruling Germany "by the will of the people," "according to the constitution."

THE THIRD VICTIM: FRANCE

Now Bismarck was ready to tackle France. Napoleon III reminded him of his vague promise to let France have some German territory. Bismarck refused to hear of it. He even refused to let France have the tiny duchy of Luxembourg, which Napoleon claimed.

Napoleon made threats, but Bismarck shrugged his shoulders. He was sure he could beat France in a war. For France had spent a great deal of money, and lost many of her best soldiers, in trying to set up an empire in Mexico. The Mexicans had revolted, and had driven out the French troops; and both the army and the treasury of France were in bad shape.

For a while longer, however, Bismarck pretended that he wanted peace. He even went to Paris with King William, and joined Napoleon III and the Czar of Russia in making speeches of friendship. But all the time Bismarck was planning for war.

The Prussian people were ready to go to war against France at any time. Ever since Napoleon I had humiliated Prussia, they had been dreaming of revenge. But the other German states were less anxious for trouble. In order to line them up on his side, Bismarck published an article in a French magazine, in which he put down all the claims that Napoleon III had made for German territory. These claims frightened most of the other German states into taking Prussia's part. When the King of Bavaria still objected to war, Bismarck simply bribed him with money.

He was afraid that England might support France. But he had a trump card to play with the English, too. The French ambassador to Berlin had foolishly written a confidential letter to Bismarck in which he proposed a secret treaty between France and Germany, aimed against England. Bismarck published this letter in a London newspaper. Naturally, it made the English furious at the French.

REVENGE AT LAST

Even now, however, Bismarck did not start the war. He preferred to have the French make the first move. So he tricked Napoleon III into declaring war on Prussia.

This is how he did it. At that time the throne of Spain was vacant. Some Spaniards wanted to have one of the Hohenzollern princes become their king. Bismarck really did not favor the idea. But he pretended that he did, and the French became excited and began to make threats of what they would do if Spain had a German king.

The French ambassador then asked King William for an audience to discuss the matter. The King refused the request. Then he sent Bismarck a telegram, telling what he and the ambassador had said to each other.

There was nothing particularly insulting to France in the telegram that came to Bismarck. But he changed it, so that it seemed as if King William had deliberately insulted the French nation, and gave it to the newspapers.

At this the proud French people demanded war. Napoleon was not eager to fight, but he dared not back down. He declared war.

A month later Moltke's magnificent army had driven over northern France like a steam roller. In half a dozen battles the bewildered French troops were crushed, and finally Napoleon himself was taken prisoner.

Then Prussia had her revenge. Bismarck took the provinces of Alsace and Lorraine, rich in coal and iron, away from France. The French people were forced to pay five billion francs—a billion dollars—then an unheard-of sum. And as a grand climax, the German princes held a great meeting in the French royal palace at Versailles, near Paris, and proclaimed that Germany was an Empire, and William of Prussia was her first Emperor, or "Kaiser."

BISMARCK BULLIES THE REICHSTAG

But the real ruler of the new empire was Bismarck, who had been made a prince. The world knew that Kaiser William allowed his prime minister to do as he pleased. He was not quite a dictator any more, however. In order to make the German people accept a Prussian emperor, Bismarck had had to agree to a new constitution. Under this constitution, the empire had a parliament, called the Reichstag, which was elected by the people in all the German states. Like the English Parliament, the Reichstag could say what taxes the people had to pay.

But Bismarck was able to make the Reichstag pass most of the laws that he wanted. Under the constitution he had complete control over foreign affairs, and could deal with the other nations of Europe without having to consult the Reichstag. If the members of the Reichstag objected to his demands for money, he would simply pretend that there was danger of war, and in this way frighten them into doing his bidding.

For example, once he wanted the Reichstag to pass a very expensive law enlarging the army—which meant higher taxes. Many members objected. While the argument was going on in Berlin, Bismarck gave secret instructions to his assistants. And far away on the French border something happened. A French customs officer was invited into Germany to discuss certain matters relating to duties on German goods. To his surprise, as soon as he set foot on German soil, he was arrested.

Then a rumor was spread in France that German soldiers had crossed into French territory to make the arrest. Naturally, the French became very angry, and the French newspapers printed articles denouncing the Germans.

This is just what Bismarck was waiting for. He took the articles from the Paris newspapers to the Reichstag, and read them aloud. He said they proved that France was getting ready to attack Germany, so that Germany simply had to have a larger army. The Reichstag was alarmed, and agreed to pass the new tax bills. After that, of course, the whole affair was quietly forgotten; for Bismarck had given orders to release the French official.

Actually, Bismarck did not want any more wars just then. He realized that England and Russia were alarmed at Germany's new strength, and that if she attacked any European country, a powerful alliance would form against her. He decided to work for peace.

When Russia went to war against Turkey, and it looked as if England and Austria were going to take Turkey's side, Bismarck persuaded them all to send their statesmen to Berlin to talk things over. This conference in 1878 became known as the Congress of Berlin, and it greatly added to Bismarck's fame. For not only did he manage to prevent the war from spreading, but he also got the other nations to do more business with Germany. After that everybody in Europe regarded him as a master diplomat.

THE WAR AGAINST THE CHURCH

In spite of his successes, Bismarck had his troubles, too. He increased the army and navy so much that it became harder and harder for him to obtain taxes to pay for them. The Reichstag's objections became louder every year. Bismarck was at times so angry that he put members who opposed him into jail; and he bribed newspapers to take his side. When even this did not help, he threatened to tear up the constitution and dissolve the Reichstag, as he had done years before in Prussia. However, he had no real intention of making good his threat, for he knew this would cause a great storm of protest all over Germany.

One of his problems grew out of religion. Prussia was for the most part a Protestant state. But some of the other states of the new empire, like Bavaria, were largely Catholic, and sent to the Reichstag a great many Catholic members, who formed a separate party. This party feared that Bismarck would in time attack Catholic Austria again. So when Bismarck wanted more money for the army, they voted against him. As a result, some of Bismarck's bills were defeated.

Bismarck was furious at the Catholic party. He resolved to put an end to the power of the Church in politics. With the Liberals behind him, he started to wage a kind of war on the Catholics— a war without bullets. He issued laws which destroyed most of the Church's influence in the schools, and he took away a great deal of Church property and income. Many priests who objected were imprisoned, or banished. For a while it looked as if the influence of Rome in Germany would be broken.

But it was not broken. The Catholics of Germany were furious at him, and continued to elect their own members to the Reichstag. Nobody knew what was going to happen.

BISMARCK CHANGES SIDES AGAIN

Then an attack fell on Bismarck from another quarter. The Liberal party in the Reichstag, which represented mostly the German business men and lawyers and school teachers, and which had been supporting Bismarck, became unfriendly to him. For the army and the great fleet that Bismarck had built up were costing more and more money. Taxes on businesses and people in moderate circumstances were going up, and the Liberals objected.

Since the conservative landholding aristocrats had never forgiven Bismarck for leaving their party, it looked as if Bismarck would have few supporters left in the Reichstag. But once again he showed how clever he was. He turned around and made his peace with the Conservatives. He told them that if they would support the military laws that he wanted, he would pass some laws that they wanted, and which would mean more money for them.

They would have been willing enough to make this deal except that many of them were Catholics, and were upset by Bismarck's attacks on the Church. Finally he consented to stop persecuting the Church, and to give back most of the property and rights he had taken away. Thereupon the Conservatives made peace with him, and he became the leader of their party again.

THE MACHINE AGE ARRIVES

While Bismarck was transforming Germany into an empire, and while landowners and business men were squabbling over taxes and laws, a great, silent change was taking place in Germany—in fact, all over Europe and the United States, too. This change is of the greatest importance, not only to the story of Bismarck, but to the lives of all of us today; and so we shall leave the "Iron Chancellor" for a moment to describe the coming of what is called the "Machine Age."

Not long before Bismarck's day, the steam-engine had been invented. Railroads began to be built. Other new machines were invented. Soon things that had taken a man working by hand many hours to make—things like carriage wheels, or knives, or shirts—could be made in a few minutes with the help of a machine.

And men also found that they could make things even faster if they worked together, and divided up the work, so that each man had to do only one thing. For instance, if they were making slippers, instead of one man making the whole slipper, he would simply stamp out the leather for the soles with a machine, and another man would cut out the cloth for the "uppers" with another machine, and a third man would stitch the soles and uppers together with a sewing machine. Soon business men were bringing workmen together by the hundreds in factories, where they could divide their labor in the way that made most slippers, or whatever the product was, per hour.

People now bought more things than ever before. For products like shoes and shirts and knives were much cheaper than they had been. And everybody wanted to own the hundreds of wonderful new things that were being made—from mechanical toys to window shades.

Business men who had enough money to put up a factory to make some article that people wanted found that they could usually sell a great deal of whatever they made at a good profit. Many of them became rich quickly. If they needed more money to build their factories, wealthy aristocrats would gladly lend it to them, and take shares in the factories, so as to become richer. Soon thousands of factories were springing up all over Europe, and there was a great "boom" in business.

THE RISE OF LABOR

Of course, these new factories had to employ millions of work-men. Most of these workmen came from peasant families which had no land. They were hired men and day laborers for farmers who owned land. In feudal days, they would have been serfs.

Their work in the country was hard and uncertain, and paid them scarcely enough to live on. When they had the chance to go to a town, and get fairly steady work in a factory, they took it. In Germany, as in France and England and the United States, there was a great movement of landless men from the farms to the factories.

Soon, however, so many of these former peasants were looking for work that there were not enough jobs to go around. In all the cities of Europe, there were hungry and desperate men who would work for any wages, no matter how small.

Some men who owned factories did not at all mind this state of affairs. For now they could say to their workmen, "Look here, you must work longer and harder, and take less money. If you don't, I'll kick you out and hire one of these unemployed fellows in your place."

Naturally, the employed workmen were not happy about hav-ing to work under such conditions. So they figured out a way to protect themselves. They formed unions, and agreed to act all together. Then they would say to their employer, "If you try to make us work longer, we will all go on strike together." Some-times they would say, "Unless you pay us higher wages, we will call a strike."

The factory owners were not anxious to have all their workmen go on strike at the same time, because it is not easy to hire a great many new men and train them all at once. So frequently they gave in to the unions. Then the unions became more and more powerful, until the business men feared and hated them. Soon there were strikes and labor troubles all over Germany—in fact, all over Europe and the United States—as workmen tried to obtain higher wages and better working conditions from employers, and employers resisted.

The wages of the workmen were for the most part very low. Most of them lived in cheap tenement houses and in dirty slums, had to pay high prices for food, and had very little pleasure in life. On the other hand, the employers often found that if they paid higher wages, they could not make as much profit as they felt they were entitled to in return for their investment and their work in getting the factory started and directing it.

LABOR GROWS RESTLESS

In Germany, the labor unions became very large and powerful. And when the German workmen had to vote in the elections for the Reichstag, they did not see the sense of voting for either the Conservatives or the Liberals. A good many of them decided to have a political party of their own that would look after their interests.

The workmen tried to figure out what kind of laws would be best for them. Many of them felt that the government ought to take the factories and the big estates away from the business men and landowners. Their idea was that all businesses and all the land should be run by the government. They thought that everybody who worked should receive wages from the government, whether he ran a factory, or tilled the soil, or dug in a mine, or wrote for a newspaper. They said it was wrong for business men to grow rich by buying things for a small price and selling them at a big price. Their ideas of government became known as Socialism.

Many Socialists thought that the workmen should try to win the elections and could gradually take the land and factories away from the capitalists. This workmen's party became known as Social-Democrats.

Then there was another, smaller party of Socialists which said there was only one way for the workmen to get control, and that was by making a revolution and seizing the government by force. This radical party received the name of Communists. They also believed that every worker in a country should receive the same wages, and have the same privileges, no matter what work he did, whether he was a diplomat, or ran a factory, or dug ditches.

As the Socialists became stronger and stronger in Germany, both the Conservatives and the Liberals were alarmed. They turned to Bismarck, and he promised to destroy the Socialist party. His chance came when some conspirators—not Socialists —tried to kill the aged Emperor William. Bismarck pretended that they were Socialists, and used the incident as an excuse to pass a new law, which put an end to all Socialist meetings and newspapers. Then he threw the Socialist leaders into prison. But he did not quite dare to break up the labor unions, because he feared a revolution if he tried it.

THE NEW KAISER

Although Bismarck was growing old, he was a proud man, and would not let anyone else have anything to say about the policies of the empire. Naturally, he had enemies, younger men who were jealous of his power, or who disagreed with him. But he was able to disregard them, because Kaiser William trusted him and no one else.

Then, in 1888, Kaiser William died, at the age of ninety-one. And there came to the throne William II, a young man who had ideas of his own. William II admired Bismarck, but he had no intention of being told what to do. He knew the story of Richelieu and Louis XIII, and he was resolved not to play second fiddle to his own minister.

In 1890 the labor unions demanded that the Socialist party be allowed to hold public meetings. Bismarck refused. But Kaiser William took the side of the workmen, because he wanted to be popular with his people. Bismarck was furious. Determined to teach the Kaiser a lesson, he gave orders that no other minister could talk with the Kaiser except when he himself was present. For he did not believe that the Kaiser would dare to dismiss him from office.

He had misjudged the new emperor. William II was proud and haughty. He called Bismarck to him, and practically ordered him to resign.

Bitterly, grudgingly, Bismarck obeyed. The Kaiser tried to appease him. But the masterful old man never forgave his royal master. He had made Germany an empire—and was this his reward? Retiring to his castle in the country, he warned that there was trouble ahead for Germany.

Then he turned away from everybody. He would sit by himself for hours at a table in the great hall of his gloomy castle, smoking his pipe, lost in visions of the past and future. In 1898 he died at the age of eighty-three, a lonely old man.

As he had foretold, there was trouble ahead. Sixteen years later, under the policies of William II, Germany had to fight an alliance of France, England, Russia, Italy, and the United States —the very war that Bismarck had wanted to avoid. Since then, as the last chapter of this book tells, life has been difficult for most of the German people.

Mussolini

Mussolini Strikes against Democracy

I N a little town in Italy, in the year 1883, the wife of a black-
smith named Alessandro Mussolini gave birth to a child—
a boy. The father and mother were both delighted at having
a son, and began to discuss what name to give him. The mother, a
religious woman, wanted a saint's name like Pietro, or Paolo.
But the father had his own idea. "The boy," he declared, "shall
be named Benito—after the great Mexican revolutionary and
democrat, Benito Juárez."

For in those days, the name of Juárez was famous among lovers
of democracy. And Alessandro Mussolini was an ardent democrat and Socialist. He was the head of a labor union in his town,
and he believed that the Italian working men and peasants ought
to overthrow the monarchy which allowed a small class of men
to gobble up the wealth of the country.

THE YOUTH OF A SOCIALIST

Little Benito Mussolini grew up hearing a great deal about
Socialism and revolution. It is said that one day when he was
eleven years old, his mother heard him screaming in his room,
and rushed to him. "Benito!" she cried. "What's the matter?"

179

"Don't interrupt, Mother!" he said. "Can't you see I'm making a speech to the workers?"

His family sent him to a Catholic school, where he often got into trouble because he would not obey his teachers. He was a quick student, however, and eventually went to a normal school. At the age of eighteen he was graduated as a teacher, and began to teach in a little school in the country.

His work bored him. And he knew that in a few months he would have to serve in the army, as all Italian young men were required to do. So he gave up his job and went to Switzerland, where the labor unions were demanding new rights for the workmen.

In Switzerland he got his first job as assistant to a bricklayer on a house that was being built. He had to work eleven hours a day, for which he received about ninety cents. The first day he had to make 120 trips from the ground to the second story, carrying a full load of bricks.

Although he was a sturdy lad, that night his muscles were so sore and swollen that he could not touch his arms. He was too tired to eat. Next morning he had to rise at five o'clock to go to work. At the end of three days he was unable to stand it any longer. He told the builder he was quitting, and the man angrily flung some coins at him.

From that point on Mussolini worked as hard as he could to help the Swiss trade unions get shorter hours and better pay for the workmen. He had jobs from time to time, but he was always fired, for his employers were furious when they heard him preaching Socialism to his fellow-workers.

In those days he was a bitter and very dissatisfied young man.

But he was sensible enough to know that the more education a man has, the better his chances of success in life. He found time to attend lectures at a Swiss university, and learned to speak French fluently. He also studied economics—which was of great importance to him later on.

His revolutionary speeches to the workers irritated the Swiss business men, who reported him to the police. One day policemen came to Mussolini's room, and ordered him to leave Switzerland at once. There was nothing to do but return to Italy. No sooner had he set foot in his own country than the military authorities sent him off to do his army service.

For a year Mussolini was a private in an Italian infantry regiment. When he was released, he very soon got into trouble again. In part of Italy the peasants were rebelling against the landholders, and demanding higher wages. Mussolini decided to help them. The police promptly arrested him as a trouble maker and threw him in jail. Presently they let him out, but after that they kept their eye on him.

By now the year 1908 had gone by; he was twenty-five years old, penniless, and out of a job. He actually thought of going to the United States to find work as a laborer, but did not have enough money to pay his passage. Then some of his friends advised him to go to a town in Austria, where there were many Italians. There he was given a job writing for an Italian Socialist newspaper, for he wrote in a bold, interesting style. In time, however, he wrote some articles saying that part of Austria rightfully belonged to Italy. The Austrian government was annoyed. As in Switzerland, the police told him to get out; so back to Italy he went.

THE "RED WEEK"

At that time the Italian parliament and government were controlled by the Liberals (which was much like the German Liberal party in Bismarck's day). In the year 1911, the government
decided to go to war against Turkey, in order to conquer the
province of Tripoli, in North Africa. Mussolini objected loudly.
In his newspaper he attacked the government for starting an unnecessary war and causing the death of thousands of young
Italians. Why were they doing it? he asked. Merely to help a few
men make money in Tripoli. The Italian workmen and peasants
would get no benefit from owning Tripoli. Italy did not need to
be a great empire. Rather, let her be a nation of culture, wealth,
and freedom. (It is worth remembering these ideas, and com-
paring them with what Mussolini himself did many years later,
in Ethiopia.)

Finally Mussolini made a speech, in which he urged Italians
not to join the army. The police seized him at once, and he was
sent to jail again, this time for five months. When he came out,
he was hailed by his Socialist friends as a martyr. Boldly he continued to attack the government.

By this time he had become such an exciting speaker that large
crowds would gather to hear him. On one hot, sultry day he was
speaking to a crowd in the open air. After an hour and a half, he
began to fear that the people were growing restless.

"Shall I stop?" he asked them.

"No, no. Go on! Go on!" they shouted. They stayed silent
while he spoke to them for another hour, and at the end they
cheered him wildly.

The Socialist party decided to reward him for his efforts by appointing him to be editor of its most important newspaper, called *Avanti,* which means Forward. He was a good editor, and more and more people began to read *Avanti.* Soon he was regarded as one of the leaders of the Socialist party. People began to speak of him as "the coming man."

In 1914, a wave of strikes broke out all over Italy. Workers and peasants put down their tools, and said they would not work again until they were given what they wanted. Aristocrats and business men thought that the Socialist revolution was really beginning.

But the labor unions were not sure just what kind of government they wanted, and while they were arguing about it, their chance of winning the strike went by. Many of the strikers' families were becoming hungry. Wives urged their husbands to go back to work. Workmen who wanted to call off the strike began to fight with workmen who wanted to go on with it. Mobs of desperate men began to roam the streets and break into shops to obtain food and clothing. Then the government told the army and police to clear the streets and forbid any public meeting of strikers. Some workmen were shot, and the rest were so discouraged that they soon gave in, and agreed to go to work again at the same old wages. This was the end of the so-called "Red Week."

Mussolini was terribly disappointed because the Socialists had not seized the government. But he had learned something—that in times of trouble a party needs strong leaders and definite ideas and bold action in order to take power. Later, as you will see, he used this lesson to become the master of Italy.

MUSSOLINI OPPOSES WAR

Soon after the Red Week of 1914, Germany and Austria went to war against France, England, and Russia. Italy had a treaty to help Germany. Mussolini wrote an article entitled "Our Neutrality Must be Absolute!" Finally the Italian government decided to tear up the treaty with Germany, and said, "We are neutral"; and Mussolini and the Socialists were delighted.

But Italy was not neutral long. The fact was that the wealthy Italians did not want to fight on Germany's side. They were afraid that the English navy would blockade Italy. But they were quite willing to fight on the Allied side. And the Italian army generals also wanted to help the Allies, because they wished to conquer their old enemy, Austria, and get Austrian territory.

The Socialists objected to helping the Allies just as much as to helping Germany. Mussolini was one of the loudest objectors. All through the summer of 1914, he wrote articles and made speeches against war. On September 21 he made a speech, in which he thundered, "Italian workers, resist the war menace!"

And then, four days later, on September 25, he amazed everybody by announcing in *Avanti* that he had changed his mind. He said that Italy should help the French against Germany.

MUSSOLINI QUARRELS WITH THE SOCIALISTS

What caused this sudden change? A great many people think they know. At that time, the French government was spending money freely to bribe Italian newspaper editors to help France. And Mussolini, who had always been poor, seemed all at once to have a lot of money. When the Socialists attacked him as a bribe-taker and a traitor, he simply resigned as editor of *Avanti,* and founded a good-sized paper of his own. After that, he helped the French cause every day. The Socialists expelled him from their party. There was so much bitterness between him and his former friends that one of them challenged him to a duel, and wounded him slightly.

But it would be foolish to think that Mussolini changed his politics just for money. The reason lies deeper than that.

Deep down in his heart he had become too ambitious to care very much about such things as democracy, or equality, or justice, or peace, which were the slogans of Socialism. In fact, he despised those who believed in democracy, for he felt that in all govern-ments a few people ruled the rest, no matter what name the government had. He wanted to be one of the rulers.

If the Socialists had been successful, he would have stayed a Socialist. But the failure of the Red Week made him feel there was not much chance for the Socialists to win in Italy—not for many years. And he did not want to wait. He wanted action—change. In the outbreak of the war he saw an opportunity to gain power. If a great many people would be killed and crippled and starved—well, it was too bad, but that was life—so he told him-self. He, Benito Mussolini, would get his chance, anyway.

THE PATRIOT

He still called himself a Socialist. But most of his attention was given to making the Italian workmen patriotic. "We are all Italians and only Italians!" he cried. Since a great many other newspapers were also telling the people that Italy must fight for her glorious name, the people soon began to believe it. In April 1915 Italy went to war.

Mussolini himself enlisted at once as a private in the infantry, and fought for two years. His admirers say he was a brave soldier, and his enemies say he was a coward. Probably he was just about as brave as most of the soldiers who go to war, and who are ashamed to admit that they are afraid, so that they fight well. He became a corporal, and finally, in 1917, he was wounded when an Italian field gun exploded near him, and pieces of metal entered his legs.

When he was well again, he returned to his newspaper. The Italian army had been badly defeated by the Autrians in the terrible battle of Caporetto, and Italy was very discouraged. Mussolini wrote many articles trying to keep up the spirit of the people.

He was particularly worried about what would happen when the war ended. For there had just been a violent revolution in Russia, whose army had been defeated by Germany. The Czar had been overthrown, and the Communist party, which believes in revolution by violent means if necessary, had come into power. This revolution had greatly encouraged Socialists all over the world.

In some of his beliefs at this time Mussolini was close to the Communists. But the Communists wanted Socialism with equality for everybody, and Mussolini did not believe in equality. Besides, the Communist leaders hated and feared him for personal reasons. So instead of working together, they fought each other bitterly.

ITALY IS RESTLESS

The Communists, Mussolini knew, were just waiting until the soldiers returned from the front, to go back to their jobs. The soldiers would be furious at the old government on account of all the suffering they had endured; and many of them would not be able to get their old jobs back, and would be unemployed and miserable. All this discontent might enable the Communists to make a revolution.

Mussolini wanted to prevent this from happening. When Germany and Austria finally surrendered to the Allies, he decided that the time had come to have a party of his own. He brought together about 150 friends who had been in the army, and they founded a political club, which he called *Fascio di Combattimento*—"fighting group." The word *fascio* really means a bundle, or bunch.

This tiny new party was as radical as the Communists in some respects. It wanted to give the workmen higher wages and shorter working hours—to take away all Church property and give it to the people—to take away most of the wealth of the business men and aristocrats and give it to the government, which would be controlled by the workmen and peasants. To the more moderate Socialists this sounded crazy. They called Mussolini "worse than a Communist." And the Communists regarded him as a fool for not joining their stronger party.

The workmen in general, no matter what their politics, were suspicious of Mussolini. When he ran for parliament, he was badly defeated. But he went on preaching revolution, and encouraging workmen to strike. In particular he aided a successful strike of the railway workers.

D'ANNUNZIO AND MUSSOLINI

In addition to labor troubles, another great problem was disturbing Italian minds. France and England refused to give Italy much of the territory won in the war. The Italians were furious. Everybody said the liberal politicians who were running the Italian government were weak. Finally one Italian decided that if the government could not get a fair share of the spoils of war for Italy, he would do something about it himself.

This man was the remarkable Gabriele d'Annunzio—aristocrat, poet, novelist, aviator, and war hero. In 1919, d'Annunzio got together several thousand Italian soldiers, just returned from the war, and led them to the Austrian city of Fiume, which France and England were about to give to Yugoslavia. Although the Allies protested, d'Annunzio took possession of the city. He said he would stay there and defend it until it became part of Italy. The Italian government was angry at having a private citizen take matters into his own hands like this, and ordered him to get out. He refused, calling them cowards.

The government could not do much about it, because the Italian people were on d'Annunzio's side. The people were delighted. Although Fiume did not mean much to them one way or the other, the whole affair was like a play; and d'Annunzio, who wrote plays, knew just what to say to make the audience applaud. Finally the Allies settled the affair by making Fiume "a free city"—which meant that the Italians would really control it. D'Annunzio went home in triumph.

While all this was going on, Mussolini was writing articles in favor of d'Annunzio, whom he greatly admired. And d'Annunzio was interested in Mussolini's new party. He helped Mussolini raise money, and when he left Fiume, most of his soldiers joined the *Fascisti,* and set up new fighting groups in cities all over Italy, under Mussolini's orders.

The Italian government was furious, and had Mussolini arrested on the charge of "conspiracy." But his followers objected so loudly that the government changed its mind and promptly let him go again. For some months he devoted himself to training his men. He worked tremendously—eighteen or twenty hours a day. For days at a time he did not take time to eat more than bread and sausage—which was very bad for his health. On one occasion he was so overworked and irritable that he put a pistol on his desk, and shouted at his assistant, "Don't let anyone come in here! I'll shoot the man who disturbs me!"

D'Annunzio and some others helped Mussolini decide on the "Blackshirt" uniform, the Roman salute, the emblem, songs, and slogans of the party. Mussolini was always a little envious of the poet. In his spare time he wrote novels and plays like d'Annunzio's, but not as good. (As late as 1939 he produced a play called *Caesar,* in which he tried to show that Julius Caesar was really very much like Benito Mussolini.) He also found time to play the violin, an instrument of which he is passionately fond.

MUSSOLINI TURNS AGAINST THE LABOR UNIONS

In 1920, the important business men of Italy decided not to pay any higher wages to the labor unions. Then the labor unions declared a general "sit-down" strike. The workmen occupied the factories and said they would not work, or let the business men hire anybody else to run the machines, until wages were raised. At first the strike was orderly, but as days went by, the strikers became uneasy, and there was some violence. The peasants and shopkeepers of Italy began to turn against the workmen. Finally the government managed to get the employers to grant a small increase in wages, and persuaded the labor unions to go back to work. But nobody was satisfied.

During this strike Mussolini was always on the side of the workmen. He said they ought to seize the government by force, and forget all about the cautious Socialist party. He hinted that if they would accept him as their leader, he would use his party to capture power for them. The workmen, however, were mostly Social-Democrats and Communists, and did not trust Mussolini. If they had satisfied his ambitions by allowing him to lead them, the whole history of Italy and of Europe would probably have been very different.

So bitter was the feud between the Socialists and the *Fascisti* that many workmen looked upon Mussolini as a kind of devil. But his powerful personality nevertheless attracted men of all kinds to him. The story goes that one angry Socialist laborer decided to assassinate him, and managed to get into his office. Once there, however, and face to face with his intended victim, who sat quietly staring at him, the man broke down. He threw his revolver on Mussolini's desk, and buried his face in his hands.

Mussolini, who knows how to make generous gestures, clapped the would-be murderer on the back, took him to dinner, and gave him his railroad fare to go back home. For he knew that he had won another recruit for Fascism.

Suddenly Mussolini changed his mind about the strikers and

the labor unions. He talked with the leaders of Italian business, and, it seems, made a deal with them. He now had more funds than ever before, and was able to persuade more men to join his Blackshirt *Fascisti* until soon there were 500,000 of them.

The first proof of his change of heart came late in 1920. A peasants' strike broke out in the south of Italy. The strikers demanded that the big landowners pay them higher wages for their work on the farms. They were marching in the streets of a town when suddenly squads of uniformed *Fascisti* attacked them. The *Fascisti* had clubs and revolvers, and the unarmed, undisciplined peasants were no match for them.

The police stood by without interfering, while the peasants were beaten up. The *Fascisti* had a trick of surrounding one or two peasants at a time, and making them drink a whole bottle of castor oil—which was a very painful form of torture. The strike broke up. The peasants went back to work at the old wages, and the landowners were delighted.

THE IDEAS OF FASCISM

A few days later, all over Italy, meetings of Socialists and Communists were attacked in the same way. Next, a railway strike was broken, and the workmen beaten until they resumed work—the same workmen whom Mussolini had urged to strike a year earlier.

Of course, he had to find a reason for his change of politics— a reason that would sound good. He could not say, "I am ambitious," or "The conservatives paid me money." Instead he called a meeting of his party, and announced a new program.

In this program he forgot all about taking the wealth away

from the owners of factories and land. He forgot about higher wages for workmen. His new ideas were that every citizen had to obey the state; and that no strikes could be permitted; that Socialism must be crushed; that parliament must give up its power; and that only a strong man, like Mussolini, was fit to rule Italy, and make her the mighty empire which she ought to be.

He also changed the name of the party, calling it the National Fascist party. When elections were held for a new parliament, the Fascist party was able to elect some members, while the Communists had fewer votes than before. But the *Fascisti* were still not by any means so large a party as the Social-Democrats, or the Liberals, who still controlled the government.

THE MARCH ON ROME

The Socialists and labor unions were now afraid that Mussolini would try to seize the government by force. They called another general strike. But the strike was quickly crushed by the Fascist "strong-arm squads." By now not only the Italian business men, but the aristocrats and the army generals, too, and even some members of the royal family, were willing to make terms with Mussolini if he would break up the labor unions once and for all.

In the autumn of 1922, he assembled an army of Blackshirts, and told them to march on Rome. At the same time, he demanded that the Italian government and parliament give up their power to him.

Even now it seemed for a while as if parliament would resist. There was some talk of calling out the army to defend Rome against the *Fascisti*. But the ministers at the last moment proved weak, and the Blackshirts entered the city unopposed.

Next, the King of Italy, Victor Emmanuel III, who did not really like Mussolini, was forced to appoint the Fascist leader prime minister. Mussolini promptly appeared before parliament, told the members that if they opposed him he would send them home or to jail, and bullied them into giving him the powers of a dictator.

Almost at once he gave his Blackshirts orders to arrest his enemies, especially the leaders of the labor unions and of the Socialist party. About 18,000 Italians were seized and sent to jail, or to some islands in the Mediterranean which were equally unpleasant. Many of these opponents of the *Fascisti* were beaten, and some killed.

Mussolini came to power because he had a strong, disciplined party of fighting men, and a definite plan for governing Italy; because the big business men were backing him, and because everybody in Italy was sick of the uncertainty and distress of the times. The King, the landholders, the Church, and even some of the peasants and workmen themselves, were so tired of their endless quarrels that they were willing to give him a chance to rule the country, if he could.

MUSSOLINI WINS WORLD RESPECT

During the next few years the other countries of the world watched Italy curiously. What kind of government was this Fascism? What kind of ruler was this Mussolini?

In the United States some people began to speak well of him. "Look," they were saying, in 1926, "he is making the Italian trains run on time for a change. He has forced Yugoslavia and the League of Nations to give the city of Fiume officially to Italy.

He is making Italy a respected nation again. When Greek bandits killed some Italians, he sent warships to bomb and capture the Greek island of Corfu. He forced Greece to pay Italy a large sum of money. Most important of all, he has reduced the taxes of Italian business men and landowners, and is letting them make big profits; and Italy is more prosperous than she has been in years."

Some of these Americans were so enthusiastic about Fascism that they said, "What America needs is a Mussolini"—meaning that we ought to have a dictator, too. Some of the great American banking houses lent a vast sum of money to the new Italian government, to help it along.

Diplomats and journalists who spoke with Mussolini were impressed by his force and keen mind. His speeches to the *Fascisti* were exciting even for foreigners, for they were full of faith that Italy would become a great and powerful empire, like ancient Rome. In photographs and motion pictures Mussolini, in his uniform, and with flashing eyes and iron jaw, stirred the imagination of everybody who admires strong men—and who does not?

THE OTHER SIDE OF THE PICTURE

In Italy, too, he became more and more popular, particularly among the youth of the country, who were thrilled by his flaming speeches about war and glory. But slowly people, particularly the poorer people, began to realize that there was another side to the picture.

Gone were the days when Italians could say what they pleased about their government. A Fascist spy system now covered the country, and those who dared speak even a word against Mussolini and the *Fascisti* might be arrested, beaten, and jailed at any time.

No longer had the people any parliament to which they could complain when they were treated unjustly. Formerly when crooked mayors and policemen had stolen money in a town, or had bullied helpless people, the indignant citizens could complain to parliament, which would look into the matter, and punish the guilty persons. But now, if the guilty men were *Fascisti*, no one dared complain about them. For the all-powerful Fascist party did not want to hear accusations against its members, and might send a squad to beat up the accuser.

In the early years of Mussolini's rule, a few bold spirits in parliament tried to hold on to the shreds of Italian liberty. One of these, a young Socialist named Matteotti, made some brilliant speeches in which he proved that Mussolini's assistants were taking public money for themselves, were beating up and murdering their opponents, and were making teachers and professors in schools and universities tell lies to their students—lies favorable to the *Fascisti,* of course.

Presently Matteotti's body was found, murdered. Mussolini said that he was "horrified." When the guilty men were finally arrested, they turned out to be gangsters who were working for the *Fascisti;* and they were let off with light jail sentences. At the same time, the *Fascisti* beat up or killed any newspaper editors who dared write articles against them.

Then Mussolini decided to use other methods. He abolished all political parties except the *Fascisti*. Parliament was turned into a "debating society," with only Fascist members, who jumped when Mussolini snapped his fingers, and said only what he permitted them to say. He made it a crime for an editor to print any articles or news not approved by the government. He also made it a crime to belong to any secret society, such as the Freemasons.

THE PICTURE BECOMES DARKER

Mussolini knew, of course, that no dictator can hold power long without a strong army. From the beginning of his rule he began to enlarge the Italian army, and buy guns and airplanes, and build tanks and warships, and construct factories to make more tanks and airplanes and ships. Of course, this cost an enormous amount of money. So, as was to be expected, he made some new tax laws. At first, he lowered the taxes on the property of wealthy people, because he did not want to make them his enemies. But he put new taxes on such things as sugar, coffee, tobacco, salt, and matches—things that everybody needs, poor people as well as rich. And since in most countries there are fifty times as many poor people as there are wealthy people, the poor provided most of the money, as well as the men for Mussolini's army and navy.

He had promised the big business men who had given him their support to put an end to the labor unions. As soon as he felt that his secret police and Blackshirt militia were strong enough to prevent any trouble, he passed a law abolishing all unions. The workmen in every industry had to join new associations run by the *Fascisti,* who decided what wages the men should receive, and how long they should work.

These Fascist associations lowered the wages of the workmen and peasants, and made them work more hours every day. A workman who had previously received two dollars for working eight hours, received a dollar and twenty cents for working ten hours. And the laborers were forbidden to strike. Strikers were regarded as criminals. From time to time the workmen held meetings to protest, but these meetings were easily broken up by the police.

Since the poor had to pay higher prices for things they bought, and had less money to buy with, naturally, they had to get along with fewer things. They had to eat less bread, less spaghetti, less butter, less sugar, less meat, less vegetables, and drink less wine and coffee. They had to live in crowded rooms, and wear the coarsest kind of clothing.

THE PEOPLE OBJECT

Il Duce (the leader), as Mussolini calls himself, is a clever and farsighted man. He knows that when people are hungry there is only one way to make them obey—and that is to make them feel that they are suffering in a good cause. History shows that there are two causes for which people willingly suffer. One is the cause of religion. The other is the cause of patriotism.

Mussolini did not care about religion. But from the beginning of his rule he took pains to make the Italian people more and more patriotic. Every child in school was taught that Italy is the finest nation in the world, and that Italians should be glad to die for their wonderful country and their *Duce*. All the children, even the very little ones, were taught to march, and carry rifles, and to want to be soldiers.

Frequently Mussolini had his army march in the cities, where the people could see them and become thrilled by the martial music and flags and uniforms and guns. He and his assistants made hundreds of speeches over the radio, and wrote thousands of articles in the newspapers, saying that Italy would soon become a great empire, like ancient Rome, and that those who complained over petty things like the price of bread were not worthy to be Italians. Naturally, Mussolini never mentioned the old days when he said that it would do Italy no good to be a great empire.

Of course, the Italians, especially the young, cheered the soldiers and the speeches, as anyone would. But as time went on, and they had less and less money to buy things with, they became restless. When were all these great happenings going to begin? When was Italy going to become a great, wealthy empire? Because if it was not going to be for a long time, they would rather have a little more to eat. Even members of the Fascist party were murmuring against the new cuts in wages, and new taxes.

Finally, in the year 1934, workmen and peasants in several towns were so miserable that they overcame their fear of punishment, and went out into the streets shouting against the tax laws and low wages. Although the police broke up the crowds, Mussolini was worried. He knew that the Italian people were becoming more and more discontented. And some of the big business men were urging him to lower wages again—which would mean more trouble.

Furthermore, Mussolini was making all the young Italian boys spend more and more time drilling and marching in the army. Mothers were lonely for their sons, and girls for their sweethearts. The people would become more and more restless, he knew, unless he gave them some more patriotic excitement, which would make them say, "This is worth suffering for!"

MUSSOLINI PREPARES FOR WAR

So he decided to give the people the only excitement that could help him—a war! He did not want a long, serious war. He wanted a short, sharp war which would thrill everybody and end in a glorious victory.

He did not dare attack any of the European countries, not even a little one, for that might bring some great power against him. His idea was to strike against a weak country which England and France would not bother to defend.

And he knew the very country. In Africa, bordering on one of Italy's colonies, was the independent kingdom of Ethiopia—a large country, but poor and backward. The Ethiopian army had only a few guns, and no airplanes or tanks. Most of the soldiers there were tribesmen, armed with spears and knives. The Ethiopian people were black, and the European countries regarded them as savages. Furthermore, the Italians hated them, for years before an Italian army had attempted to invade Ethiopia, and had been defeated and killed by the natives. But that was before the days of planes and machine guns.

First Mussolini made sure that the English and French governments would not interfere with him. These governments had promised the small nations of the world to prevent just the kind of war that Mussolini was about to make. But actually, they did not intend to carry out their promise. For one thing, they did not have enough interest in Ethiopia to fight for her. Besides, they were conservative governments, and conservatives all over the world, at that time, were sympathetic to Mussolini, and were still saying, "I wish we had a dictator in our country."

So the French and English governments secretly winked when Mussolini told them what he was going to do to Ethiopia. Later, when the war began, they protested, or pretended to protest, in order to satisfy the many Englishmen and Frenchmen who believed Mussolini should be stopped. But the governments never really intended to stop him.

ITALY MARCHES

Late in 1935, Mussolini told his army to march. The Ethiopian troops, of course, were no match for the Italian guns and planes and bombs and poison gas. In a few months, Ethiopia had been conquered, and was an Italian colony.

Italy rejoiced. True, the victory had cost a lot of money, and made life even harder for most Italians. But for a while the people forgot all about their complaints—as Mussolini knew they would.

Before the excitement wore away, he gave the people a new thrill. This time the place of action was Spain.

In Spain, a few years before, the workmen and peasants had revolted against the King, and had set up a republic, in which the Socialist and Communist parties were strong. The Spanish aristocrats and business men, the Catholic Church, and part of the Spanish army found that they were about to lose their property. So they decided to make a revolution of their own. They asked Mussolini and the German dictator, Adolf Hitler, for help, and in the summer of 1936 both Germany and Italy agreed to send soldiers and planes and artillery to help overthrow the Spanish republic. Mussolini wanted Spain to be a dictatorship, like his own, because then if he went to war against France, the Spanish dictator might help him. Besides, he wanted Italy to make a bigger profit on her trade with Spain, and that was not possible while the Spanish Republicans were in power.

This was not an easy war, for the Republicans fought fiercely. Before the Italians and Germans and Spanish Fascists could win, two years went by. Italy had to spend an enormous amount of money, and thousands of Italian soldiers were killed and wounded. However, in time the Spanish Fascists won, and set up a dictatorship much like Mussolini's, with General Franco as dictator; and they killed or imprisoned or exiled the Republican leaders. Again the Italian people cheered their *Duce*.

THE "ROME-BERLIN AXIS"

Up north in Germany, Adolf Hitler had built a mighty war machine. Since his ideas and Mussolini's were much alike, the two of them decided to form an alliance, which newspapers called the "Rome-Berlin Axis." The purpose of this alliance was to make Germany and Italy as powerful as possible, and to worry England and France as much as possible, without actually starting a war.

The way the dictators went about it was very simple. They would say they wanted something, and would go to war unless they got it. Since England and France were not ready for war and did not want to fight, they could only groan and protest while Hitler and Mussolini made threats and gobbled up territory. In this way, Italy occupied the island of Majorca in the Mediterranean, and in 1939 seized Albania, in the Balkans. Of course, these victories made Mussolini seem more wonderful than ever to the Italian people.

He encouraged the Italians to talk about attacking France, and taking away French colonies; and he tried to make as much trouble as he could for England. In Palestine, which is British territory, the Arabs and Jews were having trouble. Mussolini told the Italian radio stations to broadcast messages to the Arabs, in Arabic, telling them to fight the English and Jews together, and that Italy would help them.

To prove to the Arabs that he was on their side he attacked the Italian Jews, and took away their property. There were only a few Jews in Italy, and these were peaceful and respected citizens. Mussolini himself was once devoted to a Jewish woman, and had disapproved of Hitler's treatment of the Jews in Germany. But when it comes to politics, a dictator cannot afford to let his feelings stand in the way. He knew that it would please the Arabs and Hitler if Italy persecuted the Jews; so he did.

MUSSOLINI STAYS NEUTRAL

But Mussolini had no intention of getting into a big war unless he seemed pretty sure to win. He realized that if a French army succeeded in invading Italy, and the English fleet blockaded the country, the Italian people would become discouraged. Then, as their patriotism ebbed away, they would remember their troubles, and might revolt against the *Fascisti,* and drive him from power.

He kept careful watch as his partner, Hitler, reached out for new territory—Austria, and Czecho-Slovakia, and Danzig. Mussolini feared that if Germany went too far, war would break out; for England and France could not stand by forever and watch

Germany become the master of central Europe. Finally, when Hitler attacked Poland, England and France unwillingly went into action. But Mussolini said, "Italy is not going to fight—yet."

MUSSOLINI'S PLAN

This was wise of *Il Duce*. His idea was that Italy should sell goods of all kinds at high prices to Germany and the other countries. This would mean big profits for Italian business men and more money for the government, which he could spend for more guns and planes. In this way Italy would become stronger while the fighting nations became weaker. Then when the time came, he could join the winning side, so as to share in the spoils of war.

As Germany invaded Denmark, Norway, the Netherlands, Belgium, and France, as the war grew ever fiercer, Mussolini talked more and more loudly and threateningly against the Allies. Finally, when the French army had been crushed by the Germans, he declared war on France and England.

If Italy wins and holds on to new colonies without serious trouble, the Italian people will, of course, cheer louder than ever for their *Duce* and for the *Fascisti*. They will accept their low wages and high taxes so long as they have something to be patriotic about. But if Italy should be defeated in war, or if the war ends without much gain and business becomes bad for a long while, then the rulers of Italy had better look out. When people are hungry and their government gives them nothing to hope for —that is when revolution begins.

Meanwhile, the Italian people can only hope that *Il Duce* and the men who follow him will be kind to them. For they dare not complain; they must take what they are given. Democracy in Italy is dead, struck down by Mussolini. It is strange, is it not, to think that the man who did all this began as a fighter for the rights of the common people?

Stalin

Stalin Masters the Soviets

IN the south of Russia, at the point where Europe merges with Asia, is the rugged mountainous country of Georgia. There for centuries, until recent times, a proud and warlike people lived mainly by herding sheep and growing grain; and also by robbery, which used to be the favorite occupation of many Georgians.

In a small Georgian town, in the 1880's, a boy named Josef Djugashvilli grew up hearing tales of the famous Georgian bandits, and no doubt, like all boys, admiring their bravery and desperate fights with the Russian Cossack police. For although Georgia had become part of Russia around 1800, many Georgians hated the Russians and dreamed of having an independent country, as in the past.

Young Josef's parents were very poor; his father repaired boots, and his mother, too, worked to make a living for the family. The boy, who was intelligent, went to a little school, where he learned to read and write. Presently his father died. Then his mother decided to move to the biggest city in Georgia, Tiflis, where she had friends. It was her ambition to send Josef to a school for priests; for to be a priest seemed to her the finest career that her son could hope for.

Josef was tremendously excited at living in a large city. But he did not like his new school. The priests were strict, and made him work and study and pray, when he would rather have been out playing "bandits and Cossacks" with the other boys. Again and again he got into trouble for leaving the school without permission.

As he grew older, the trouble became more serious. He made new friends, and some of these friends held ideas which the priests disapproved of—such as that Georgia ought to revolt against Russia, and that the poor people should rebel against the rich landowners. In those days, owing to the harshness of the aristocrats, and the great poverty and distress of most other people all over Russia, there was much talk of revolution and of Socialism. Many men of independent spirit considered it their duty to conspire against the government. When the priests found that Josef was becoming a revolutionary and a Socialist, they angrily expelled him from the school, for, of course, the Russian Church was on the side of the government.

THE CONSPIRATOR

Josef was then nineteen years old. For a while he obtained work as a bookkeeper in a business concern. But his chief interest was in overthrowing the government of the Russian emperor, or Czar. He and other young men would meet secretly at night, and discuss plans for starting a revolution in Georgia. One of his friends lent him some pamphlets and articles by a Russian named Lenin, who was the leader of the Communist wing of the Russian Socialists. Josef was deeply impressed by these pamphlets, and became an ardent Socialist and a great admirer of Lenin.

At that time railroads were being built in Georgia, and oil had been discovered. Business was becoming important, and poor peasants were crowding into the cities to find work at the oil wells, or on the railroads, or in factories. As in Germany, years before, they soon started to complain against the way their employers treated them, and to form unions to protect themselves.

Josef helped the workmen to organize these unions, and led some of them in strikes for higher wages. He wrote articles and made speeches to the workers. When the Georgian business men asked the police to put down the strikes and arrest the leaders of the unions, the police tried to arrest Josef, but he escaped in time. To throw them off his trail, he began to use various disguises and assumed names; and he went on writing and speaking to the workmen, and urging them to revolt. One of his assumed names was Stalin—which means "steel." And as Stalin this Josef Djugashvilli has been known to the world ever since.

THE REVOLT IS CRUSHED

Finally the police caught him, and sent him to jail for almost two years. After that he was banished to a distant part of Russia. But he was a hard man to keep under guard, for he was quick and clever. He escaped almost at once, and again plunged into the struggle of the Russian workmen against the business men and aristocrats.

Russia had gone to war against Japan, and, to the surprise of the world, was being badly beaten. For although Russia was much larger than Japan, the men who ran the Russian government and the Russian army were for the most part weak and stupid, and were interested only in filling their own pockets. Tens of thousands of Russian soldiers were killed at the front and hundreds of thousands were wounded, or became sick as a result of eating bad food. And the workingmen and peasants at home had to pay such high taxes that they could barely squeeze a living out of their wages.

Finally the Russian people were so bitter against their government that the Socialists thought it was a good time to revolt. They held a secret conference in Finland, and Stalin's friends gave him enough money so that he could attend. There for the first time he met his hero, Lenin. Lenin was a small man, with a beard and eyeglasses, and he looked more like a college professor than a revolutionary leader. But when Stalin heard him speak, he knew that he was listening to a strong man. Although Lenin spoke very simply and quietly, his ideas were much more convincing than the ideas of others, because they were clear and logical. Stalin nick-named him "the mountain eagle of the party."

Stalin went back to Georgia, to prepare for the revolution. Presently workmen all over Russia, Georgia included, went on strike; and the Socialists demanded that the Czar abdicate, and that a republic be set up. But the Czar still had enough loyal soldiers to shoot down the unarmed strikers, and he managed to prevent the revolution from really getting started. After that the famous Cossack cavalry began to torture and shoot and imprison all those who were even suspected of being against the Czar. This was in 1905.

STALIN ROBS A BANK

Stalin, like all the Socialists, was disappointed; but he was not disheartened. He managed to escape from Russia, and to join Lenin. Lenin was making plans to try again, as soon as another chance should present itself. Meanwhile, he was in close touch with the Socialists in other countries, for Socialists believe that the workmen and peasants of all countries should stick together, regardless of what quarrels their kings and business men may have.

The other Russian Socialist leaders did not think much of Stalin. For one thing, he was not as well educated as they, and could speak no language but Russian. For another, he looked like a ruthless man, who would stop at nothing to gain his ends. But Lenin saw that Stalin might be useful to Socialism, and particularly to the Communist party, or Bolsheviks as they were called. For, as you know, the Communists, who were in favor of revolution, had no patience with the Social Democrats, who wanted to bring about Socialism gradually.

The Communist party was in desperate need of money to pay for newspapers and pamphlets. Only in this way could they tell the workmen of Russia and other countries their side of the story, and make them willing to help in the next revolution. Stalin told Lenin that he would try to get some money for him.

He went back to Georgia, to Tiflis. The police arrested him, but he escaped to the mountains. There he sought out a gang of bandits, and told them that he wanted their help—and that they would be paid for it.

For he had made a plan—to rob the largest bank in Tiflis. It was exactly the kind of plan that a man who had grown up dreaming of bandits and Cossacks would have made. Spies in Tiflis brought him word that on a certain day the cashier of the bank was going to transfer a large sum—about $170,000—from the post office to the bank.

That day the bandits came down to the city secretly, and lay in wait. Stalin saw the cashier leave the post office with a package in his hand, and enter a carriage, which was surrounded by Cossack soldiers on horseback. Suddenly one of the bandits threw a bomb under the carriage, and it went off, killing the cashier. Other bombs were thrown. As the Cossacks' horses bolted in all directions, the bandits swooped down from a nearby street, shooting and yelling. One of them, disguised as a Cossack officer, shot the carriage horses, which were running away, and grabbed the package containing the money.

It was much like a stage-coach robbery in the American "Wild West" of earlier days, but bloodier, for it is said that more than fifty Cossacks and bystanders were killed or wounded by the bomb explosions. The bandits escaped to the mountains, and divided their loot. More than half the money was sent to the headquarters of the Communist party.

Stalin's conscience was not at all troubled over this affair. He felt that he had not committed a crime—that what he had done was war—war against "the enemies of the working class." He had acted not for personal gain, but "for the revolution." All his life he has shown this same ruthlessness. He has never hesitated to kill when killing, in his judgment, would advance the cause he believed in. In this respect, he is like most strong dictators.

ARRESTS AND ESCAPES

The police caught Stalin again, and again he escaped. But finally he fell into their hands once too often. They could not prove that he was guilty of murder, but they found him guilty of political crimes, and sent him to work in the Siberian mines—a dreaded punishment. In the Siberian camp, the Cossack guards would flog their prisoners, or worse still, force them to "run the gantlet." This meant that the prisoner had to run between two long lines of Russian soldiers, who struck his head and shoulders with the butts of their heavy rifles. Lucky was the prisoner who escaped only with some broken bones and bruises, for men have died and gone mad under this ordeal.

On Easter Sunday, 1909, Stalin was forced to endure this torture. Fortunately for him, he was physically tough and brave of spirit, and he escaped without serious injury. Soon afterward he managed once again to elude his guards and get out of Russia.

Lenin then was in Austria, still working patiently for the revolution which, he was sure, must come sooner or later, as the miseries of the Russian people increased. A newspaper called *Truth* had been started by Communists in the Russian capital, St. Petersburg, and Lenin ordered Stalin to go there under an assumed name and become one of the editors. But one of Stalin's fellow-workers was really a spy for the police, and he gave away Stalin's secret.

This time the police had learned their lesson. Stalin was sent under special guard to a village far north, near the Arctic Ocean. Any attempt to escape now meant death from cold and starvation. From 1913 to 1917, Stalin lived as a hunter and fisherman.

WAR AND REVOLUTION

Little news reached Stalin in his frozen village. But every
now and then he would hear a rumor from some good-natured
guard, or newly arrived prisoner, about what was happening in
Europe. In 1914 came a startling report. A great war had begun.
Germany and Austria were fighting England, France, Italy, and
Russia. Russia was winning.

A year passed. Stalin wondered about Lenin. Where was he?
In prison? Or still working away? Another year. The rumor ran
that the Russian troops had been badly defeated by the Germans.
And then suddenly, early in 1917, came amazing news. There
had been a revolution! The Czar had given up his throne! A
republic had been set up, headed by a man named Kerensky. All
political prisoners were free to return to their homes!

Stalin rejoiced. He made his way back to St. Petersburg. There
he heard Kerensky, who was a wonderful orator, speak of "the
new freedom of Russia," and say that under the republican government the Russian army was sure to defeat the Germans. Stalin
cheered Kerensky with the rest.

The Communists whom he met said that Lenin was still in
Switzerland. What was he doing there, Stalin wondered, when
there was so much excitement in Russia? Then one day the
rumor spread that Lenin was on his way to Russia. He had been
unable to get out of Switzerland before. Finally the German
government had provided a train to take him across Germany.
The Germans knew that Lenin was opposed to war between nations. They hoped that he would persuade the Russians to stop

fighting. Then the Germans would be able to devote all their strength to attacking France.

"ALL POWER TO THE SOVIETS!"

A group of Communists, Stalin among them, decided to go to the railroad station to meet Lenin. When they saw his little figure in its shabby clothing, they cheered, and called for a speech. Lenin stood on the platform of the train and spoke to them in his usual simple, direct way. The revolution, he said, had only begun. He said that by overthrowing the Czar, Kerensky's government had only transferred power from the aristocrats to the business men of Russia. The workmen and peasants would be no better off. They should not put their faith in Kerensky's government. Instead, they should work to set up their own government. The unions in each part of Russia had elected their leaders to meet in a council known as a Soviet. Every district had its Soviet of peasants, and every city had its Soviet of workmen. These Soviets, declared Lenin, would be the beginning of a workmen's government. "All power to the Soviets!" he exclaimed.

Stalin was tremendously excited by this speech. He felt that he had made a mistake in believing Kerensky, and asked Lenin what he could do to help the Communist cause again. Lenin sent him to explain the meaning of Socialism to the peasants in the country, and also to the soldiers in the army.

For Russia was still fighting Germany, and every day thousands of Russian soldiers were being killed and wounded. Lenin felt that the war ought to stop, because he could see no sense in letting all these young Russians be slaughtered. Stalin and others smuggled pamphlets and newspapers to the soldiers asking them what they were fighting for. "Turn your bayonets against the men who are keeping you in this war," said the pamphlets.

THE COMMUNIST REVOLUTION

The Russian soldiers read the pamphlets and talked about them. They were not yet ready to revolt. They thought Kerensky was a great man, and believed him when he told them that Russia would beat the Germans. But their guns were not nearly so good as the German guns, and they did not have enough ammunition. When Kerensky ordered them to attack the German lines again, they were mowed down by the German machine guns, just as when the Czar's generals had commanded them. This time the soldiers could endure no more. They turned on their officers and mutinied, and many of them joined the Communists.

At the same time, Lenin and his men were working to win the support of the Soviets. Most of the workmen in the Soviets were Social-Democrats, and not Communists; they were opposed to a violent revolution. But Lenin, who was hiding from Kerensky's police, kept writing articles until the Soviets changed their minds. A Congress of Soviets of workmen, peasants, and soldiers from all Russia met in Petrograd (now Leningrad). Lenin suddenly appeared on the platform. He made a speech urging the Soviets to revolt against Kerensky, and set up a Socialist government. The Congress cheered him, and elected him and the Communists to direct the new government. Stalin was elected to the most important committee, which was like being a member of the President's cabinet in the United States.

The next day the Communists attacked the palace where Kerensky had his government, and captured it after some fighting. Kerensky escaped, and tried to get part of the Russian army to march on Petrograd and destroy the Communists. But the soldiers decided that they would rather fight for Lenin, and Kerensky had to fly for his life, and leave the country, never to return.

As soon as he could, Lenin made peace with Germany. He knew that he could not hope to fight the German armies. Even when the Germans insisted on taking a large part of Russia, he was willing to agree. For he was sure that Germany would in time lose the war against France, England, and the United States, and that Russia would get back her territory.

THE ALLIES PREPARE TO ATTACK RUSSIA

Meanwhile, the property of the Russian aristocrats and business men was being taken away. The factories became the property of the government, while the large landed estates were divided up among the peasants. Most of the people who had owned much property had to leave Russia, or run the risk of being killed, for the workmen and peasants were bitter against their former masters. Some of the aristocrats were treated cruelly; the Czar and his family, for instance, were shot to death. This is what usually happens in revolutions, when an oppressed people rises in wrath against its oppressors.

Naturally, the aristocrats and business men who governed the other countries in Europe were furious at the Russian Communists. Like the foreign aristocrats when the French Revolution of 1789 began, they were afraid of the example of the revolution on the workmen and peasants of their own countries. Soon all over the world newspapers and books were telling the public how terrible the revolution was.

The Communists, too, had friends and sympathizers in other countries, and they formed an "International Party." The International began to tell people how wonderful the revolution was, and how happy the free Russian people were, and what a beautiful future lay ahead for Russia, and that other countries ought to follow Russia's example. Some of them exaggerated as much as their enemies. Soon both sides were turning out "propaganda" as fast as they could. But the conservatives were by far the larger group.

THE ATTACK BEGINS

The strong feeling against the Communists in the Allied countries pleased the conservatives who controlled the governments. After 1918, when Germany surrendered, they decided to send armies to attack the Russians. There was a Polish army which attacked from the west; there were English and French armies which attacked from north and south; while Japanese and American troops landed in Siberia. Furthermore, a great many Russian aristocrats and business men and soldiers joined the attack on the Communists.

Against these odds it seemed unlikely that the Communists could survive. But somehow they did. Most of the Russian workmen and peasants felt that they were fighting in a good cause, and, like the French revolutionary troops, they fought bravely. Their commander-in-chief was a man named Leon Trotsky—a Russian Jew. (Lenin and Stalin were not Jews.) Although he had never led an army before, Trotsky proved himself an excellent general, and after some early defeats, began to drive back the invaders.

STALIN SHOWS A HARD FIST

Trotsky did not like Stalin. Lenin, however, believed in Stalin's ability, and sent him to undertake a very difficult job.

A great many people in Russia itself—lawyers, teachers, well-to-do peasants, and owners of small factories and shops—were naturally afraid that their property and jobs would be taken away from them if the Communists remained in power. They could not afford to leave Russia, so they pretended to be on the side of the Reds, or Communists. Secretly, however, they hoped that the Whites, the aristocrats' armies, would win, and they tried to help the Whites when they could, especially by spreading rumors to frighten the Red soldiers. It was Stalin's task to find these friends of the Whites and keep them quiet, so that the people who were on the Red side would not be discouraged.

The way he went about it shows how hard a fist he has. He would go into a city and organize a secret spy system of Communists. The spies would talk to the suspected Whites, and learn what they really felt about the Reds. Then Stalin would have some of the men who seemed to be on the White side brought together, and shot. This would frighten the other Whites into keeping quiet, or even joining the Reds.

It was an unpleasant job, but he did it thoroughly. People all over Russia began to fear him. And although Trotsky disliked him more than ever, there is no doubt but that Stalin's work behind the lines helped Trotsky's armies win battles. By 1922 the Whites were completely beaten, the Poles had retreated, and the Allied countries were forced to withdraw their troops.

STALIN BECOMES PARTY SECRETARY

At the end of the war with the Whites and the Allies, Lenin rewarded Stalin by making him Secretary of the Communist party. This job is much more important than it sounds. The Communist party in Russia is in many respects like the Fascist party in Italy. It is the only party permitted. To belong to it is a great privilege for a Russian, for the members of the party get all the best jobs and really run the country. Out of about 175,-000,000 Russians only about 2,000,000 are full-fledged Communists.

The Secretary of the Communist party can say who will be made a member and who will not. Naturally, he has enormous power. Most of the Communists and the Russians who hope to become Communists want to prove that they are his friends, so they do what he tells them to. It did not take Stalin long to become the most important politician in Russia, although not many people realized it.

In 1918 Lenin was shot by a dissatisfied Communist, and he never fully recovered. By 1922 he had become very ill, especially because he worked hard, trying to straighten out all of Russia's terrible problems after the war. People began to wonder who would take his place. Most Communists thought it would be Trotsky, who was still head of the army, and a close friend of Lenin. But Stalin had his own ideas.

He was quietly making friends with other leaders of the Communist movement who were jealous of Trotsky. Finally he was ready to strike. A meeting of the supreme council of the government was held, and the council voted to remove Trotsky as head of the army, and put one of Stalin's followers in his place.

Trotsky was known as a very clever, and very able man. When he realized what Stalin had done, he was furious, but he could not do anything about it. He hoped that Lenin would recover his health and denounce Stalin. But Lenin died. Still Trotsky struggled to get back his power. For he knew that Lenin had left a letter, telling his wishes about the way Russia should be governed.

When the letter was opened, Trotsky's hopes rose. The will condemned Stalin for his harsh and ruthless ways, and urged the Communists to remove him from his post as Secretary.

But by this time Stalin was too strong to be beaten even by Lenin's wishes. He said he was sorry if he had been too harsh, but that he was only doing his best for the Communist party, and that he would try to do better in the future. The Communist leaders voted that they had confidence in him, and he continued as Secretary.

Then began a long contest between Stalin and Trotsky. Trotsky had a great reputation among the Russian people as a hero of the revolution. He saw that the people of Russia were very badly off, and he believed that he could force the Communist party to give him back his power. He was a passionate speaker, and had a great talent for persuading people to do what he wanted.

STALIN AGAINST TROTSKY

It is important to understand the argument between Trotsky and Stalin, for that argument lies at the heart of modern Russian history.

At that time Russia was not completely a Socialist state as it is today. Some big businesses had been taken over by the government, and the big estates had been divided up among the poor peasants. But the peasants still owned their land, and sold their crops for as much as they could get; and the small business men still ran their businesses and made profits.

Trotsky said to the Communists that allowing the business men to continue to do business in Russia was unfair to the peasants—and most of the Russian people were peasants. He said that the peasants were worse off than they had been under the Czar. When the peasant sold his wheat and eggs and vegetables to the business man, he received just about the same amount he had made before the revolution. But when he went to buy a pair of shoes, or a suit of clothes, or a package of nails, or a dish to eat out of, he had to pay more than twice as much as in the old days. He could buy only half what he had been able to buy before, and so he was only half as well off as before.

Why were the prices of manufactured articles high? Trotsky asked. Because Russia had only a few factories of her own, and these were not well managed. She could not make the things her people needed.

Many articles which Russia wanted were for sale at low prices in Germany, England, France, and the United States. But to pay for these things the Russian government needed gold, and all the Czar's gold had been taken out of the country by the aristocrats. And the other countries would not lend money to Communists.

Most of the peasants were so poor that they had to borrow money from some well-to-do peasant, who took the poor peasant's crops in payment. These richer peasants, whom the Russians called *kulaks,* or "fists," were even getting hold of the land which the poor peasants had just received from the government.

What could be done to help the poorer peasants? Trotsky demanded. And he answered: Put an end to the private businesses once and for all, and let the government run all business. Get rid of the *kulaks*. Build a great many factories in Russia to make all the things needed, and make them cheaply. Teach Russians how to run factories properly. And begin right away.

This speech made a deep impression on the Communists. For a time it looked as if Trotsky were going to get back his power. But Stalin's friends fought back. They said it costs a great deal of money to build factories, and buy machinery, and pay wages to workmen. Where was the money to come from? Stalin's idea was to let the small business men and the *kulaks* make money for a few years longer, and then take it away from them and use it to build the factories. And the Communist party finally voted to support his policy.

TROTSKY LOSES HIS FIGHT

When Trotsky saw that the Communist party was on Stalin's side, he and his followers turned to the peasants and workmen of Russia, and began to win support for his ideas among them. Now the Communists have a rule that once the party has decided on a policy, all the members must work for that policy, even if they do not agree with it. Trotsky refused to obey this rule. He said that by encouraging the business men and *kulaks* the party was weakening Socialism in Russia, and he attacked Stalin again and again.

But Stalin was only biding his time. Suddenly, in 1927, his secret police arrested Trotsky and his followers. Stalin denounced them as traitors, and the Communist party expelled them. Trotsky was banished to Siberia, and finally was ordered to get out of Russia entirely. He went to Turkey, France, Norway, Mexico—a fugitive from the revolution he had helped to make.

The argument between Stalin and Trotsky divided the Communists all over the world into two camps, hating each other bitterly. The Russian revolution was much like the French, in the way power passed from group to group. It began with the liberal business men and the Socialists together taking power away from the aristocrats. Then the Communists took the power away from the liberals and Social-Democrats. Finally the Stalinist Communists took power away from the Trotskyite Communists.

At this point Stalin became the unquestioned dictator of Russia. Although his only title was still that of Secretary of the Communist party, the party did what he wanted done, and the Soviets did what the party wanted, and the people as a whole did what the Soviets wanted. Those who dared to disobey soon found that Stalin's dreaded secret service was on their trail.

THE FIVE-YEAR PLAN

One of Stalin's sayings is, "Learn from everybody—from your enemies—from your friends—but particularly from your enemies." And as soon as Trotsky was out of the way, Stalin began to use some of Trotsky's ideas. He undertook a great Five-Year Plan to give Russia some of the railroads and factories that the backward country needed, and to bring Socialism to the Russian peasant. Later, there was a second and a third Five-Year Plan.

He went about it just as ruthlessly as he robbed the bank in

Tiflis. First he took away all the money, goods, and grain supplies of the small business men and *kulaks*. Then he sold the
grain in other countries, and bought machinery with the money.
Even peasants who were not *kulaks* were forced to give up most
of their wheat to the government. If they resisted, the Red soldiers shot them. Millions of peasants tried to fool the government
by planting only enough wheat for their own families. But Stalin
refused to allow them to keep wheat for themselves unless they
had some for Russia, and took away their private supply. Even
pigs and cows were taken by the government. As a result, a great
many poor peasants starved to death—and hundreds of thousands of small business men and *kulaks* also starved, or drifted
away to try to find some kind of work.

Furthermore, all over Russia peasants were made to give up
their little patches of land and go to work on big "collective
farms," where they worked in large groups, and where they were
really wage laborers for the government. Probably in the long
run they gained by the change. On the collective farms they use
tractors and modern machinery which they never had before, so
their work is less back-breaking, while their life is more interesting and more secure, because they live in larger and better educated groups. But the desire to own land of his own is strong in
the peasant the world over, and at first the Russian peasants resisted as hard as they could. As a result many of them were shot
or turned out to starve by the stern Red soldiers.

Meanwhile the government was building factories, railroads,
dams for generating electricity, schools for training workmen.
For a time it seemed as if there was hope of transforming Russia
in a few years into a modern country, with workmen and peasants better off than they had ever been. All the world watched

with interest. Business men in England, France, Germany, and the United States became eager to trade with the Russians, even though they still hated the idea of Communism.

GUNS OR SHOES?

About 1935, however, it became clear that something was going wrong with the Russian plan. The workmen in the factories and on the collective farms still were receiving low wages, and still had to pay high prices if they wanted shoes, or butter, or cigarettes. Most Russians were no better off than they had been before the Five-Year Plan. People started to complain, and to ask, "What is the trouble?"

Part of the trouble arose, of course, because it is impossible to turn a nation of peasants into a nation of industrial workers in a few years. It took Japan fifty years, and the Japanese were quicker than the Russians in learning how to use machines.

But there is an even more important reason why the Russian people have not been able to get better food, and clothing, and houses to live in. That reason is the famous Red Army.

Stalin did not have the money or the trained men to build all the factories and railroads he would have liked to build. If he built a factory here, that meant he could not build one there for a long time to come. If he built factories to weave cloth for women's dresses, he might have to get along without a steel mill, or a railroad line. So he had to decide which factories were most important.

One thing he was pretty sure about was that the other governments of Europe and the government of Japan were still Russia's enemies. He believed that Socialist Russia would some day have to defend itself against an attack. This is how he reasoned: "What good will it do the Russian people to build shoe factories if the other countries will afterward drop bombs on them, or capture them and turn them back to private owners? Our first job is to make sure that won't happen. We must have an army and an air force so strong that no nation will dare to attack us."

He ordered that more factories be built for making airplanes, tanks, guns, submarines, and all the other things that a strong military nation requires. Naturally, this meant that the factories for making clothing, canned foods, and woodwork for houses could not be built. So most of the Russian people had little more comfort and pleasure in life than they had in the days of the Czar, although they had a stronger army.

TERROR SWEEPS RUSSIA

After Adolf Hitler came to power in Germany Stalin became more and more alarmed, for he feared that Germany would attack Russia from the west, and Japan from the east, at the same time. He built up the Red Army even faster. This meant that millions of young Russians had to be fed and clothed and paid while they were being drilled. The rest of the Russian people had to work harder and get along with skimpy wages, and to pay special taxes in order to keep the army going.

When the Russian people found that the goods they wanted were as scarce and expensive as ever, and their wages were no higher, they began to complain that the Communist party was not keeping its promises. They saw that although nobody in Russia was allowed to get rich, a good many Communist officials were having a much better life than the workmen or peasants had—living in better houses, wearing better clothes, riding around in government automobiles. Some Russians began to feel that the Communist party was only looking out for itself and the army, and not caring very much about the other 170,000,000 workers.

Furthermore, Leon Trotsky, in far-off Mexico, still had his friends in Russia, and still was writing articles denouncing Stalin. He said that Stalin was not a true Socialist—that he was a blood-thirsty Georgian bandit, who was concerned only with his own authority. The Communist party, he went on, had become a ruling class almost as selfish as the Czar's aristocracy. He said that Russia ought to get rid of Stalin and elect a government that would do what the people wanted.

It appears that Trotsky's writings were smuggled into Russia, and that some of his friends organized a conspiracy to overthrow Stalin's government. One of Stalin's chief lieutenants was ac-tually murdered. At this Stalin became furious. It is said that in his rage he himself actually beat up a Russian official whom he considered at fault. His secret police began to arrest everybody who was even suspected of being against him. Thousands of Russians were imprisoned, sent to Siberia, or shot. A wave of terror swept the country. People were so afraid of spies that they dared not open their mouths to say a word about politics. Every man suspected his neighbor of being a government spy.

STALIN GIVES RUSSIA A "CONSTITUTION"

Finally a number of important men in the Communist party itself were arrested, charged with treason, tried, and shot. Stalin said that the trials of these men, which were made public, proved that the troubles of his country were caused by "Trotsky's conspiracy." Trotsky denied that there had been any conspiracy. He said that the evidence was all faked, and that Stalin was just using the trials as an excuse to shoot Communists who knew the truth about him. Other students of Russian affairs believe that some of the evidence was faked, but that some kind of plot against the government actually existed.

Stalin wanted to weaken the arguments of his enemies, so in 1936 he proclaimed that Russia was going to become the most democratic country in the world. To prove it, he announced a new constitution, which was even more democratic than that of the United States. According to this constitution, the Soviets would have complete control of the Russian government, and the people would elect the members of the Soviets, with every citizen free to vote as he wished. Actually, however, this did not change anything. The Communist party in every part of Russia continued to say who could run for election to the Soviets, and who could not. The only candidates the people could vote for were Stalin's friends. As a result, the Soviets continued to be mere tools of the party and of Stalin; and Russia remains a dictatorship.

STALIN MAKES A DEAL WITH HITLER

In 1939, the war clouds hung heavy over Europe. Stalin saw that England and France would soon fight Germany. Most people thought that he was going to join in the war, and that he would be against Germany, because Hitler's government had treated the German labor unions very much as Mussolini had treated the Italian unions. Stalin knew that Hitler's Germany was an enemy of Russia and of Communism. But he also knew that the English and French governments were enemies of Communism.

He was afraid that if he joined with England and France, they would wait until the war began, and then make a truce with Hitler, and let Germany and Russia fight it out. If that happened, Stalin feared that Germany would win, because the German army was very strong, and the German factories could turn out more guns and bombs and airplanes than the Soviet factories.

Stalin felt that his most important task was to prevent Soviet Russia from being conquered. He was not going to get into a war against Germany alone if he could help it—not unless Germany had previously been weakened by fighting France and England. He encouraged England and France to believe that he might be persuaded to fight on their side. But all the time he was secretly sending Russian diplomats to Berlin to make a deal with Hitler. He knew that Hitler was not anxious to fight England and France, if Russia was likely to attack Germany at any time.

Suddenly it was announced that Nazi Germany and Soviet Russia had signed a treaty. Neither would attack the other, and they would trade with each other as much as possible.

This treaty made England and France furious at Russia, because it left them to fight Germany alone. And in every country, including the United States, many people who had been friendly to Soviet Russia became her enemies. They hated Hitler so much that they could not excuse Stalin for giving Germany any encouragement in her war with England and France.

But European statesmen know that this deal between Stalin and Hitler is not really a pact between friends. It is a truce between enemies. If either thought he could safely attack the other, he would. Meanwhile, both have something to gain by pretending to be on good terms.

RUSSIA TAKES ADVANTAGE OF THE WAR

As soon as Hitler was sure that Russia would not attack him, he told his army to invade Poland. Just why he wanted war with Poland you will read in the next chapter. Here we are concerned with the effects of Hitler's move on Russia and Stalin.

Although the English and French governments really cared little about the Poles, they had warned Hitler that if he invaded Poland they would fight him, for they were alarmed at the rapid growth of his power. But they could not do anything to help the Poles. The Germans were able to go right ahead and beat the Polish army, which was weak. Then they started to march across Poland toward Russia.

Stalin did not like the idea of having German troops so close. He believed that in spite of the "non-aggression pact," Hitler might keep right on going and invade Russia while he was at it. So the Soviet leader gave orders to the Red Army to move up to the Russian side of Poland. Then when the Polish army had been hopelessly defeated by the Germans, the Russians marched in from the east, and occupied about half of Poland. Hitler could not tell the Red Army to get out of Poland, because that would have ended the pact and meant war with Russia, while he was fighting England and France. So he had to allow Russia to keep half of Poland.

THE SOVIETS REACH FOR THE BALTIC

This was a great victory for Stalin, for the German army had had all the work of beating the Poles, and thousands of Germans had been killed; but Russia got half the spoils.

About the same time, Stalin turned his attention to three little countries on Russia's western frontier—Lithuania, Latvia, and Estonia. These countries had ports on the Baltic Sea, and Stalin feared that Russia might some day be invaded from the Baltic. He wanted to allow Russia's submarines and battleships and airplanes to use the ports of the small neighboring nations. So he said to Lithuania, "Turn these ports over to Russia, and let Russia boss your government, or the Red Army will invade you." And although many Lithuanians objected, because they feared that Russia would set up a Communist government in Lithuania, they saw it was hopeless to resist. Lithuania gave in to Russia, and Latvia and Estonia followed her example. And all over the world people started to say, "While Germany is fighting England and France, Russia is really winning the war without bloodshed."

FINLAND RESISTS

Then Russia turned to Finland and demanded that the Finns too give up to the Soviets certain islands and ports on the Baltic coast of their country. But the Finns were much stronger than the Lithuanians. They had been preparing for trouble with Russia for a long while, and had built a strong line of forts across their Russian border, and had bought from other countries the best guns they could get.

When the Finns refused the Russian demands, Stalin sent strong Russian armies to invade Finland. The Finns are excellent soldiers, and for several months held off the Russian army, killing many thousands of Russians. Meanwhile, however, Russian airplanes were dropping bombs on Finnish cities and railroads, and making it hard for the Finns to send troops and food to the battle-front. In time Russia's army broke through the Finnish defenses and Finland surrendered. As the price of peace, she had to agree to the Russian demands for territory.

When the fierce war between Germany and France and England exploded in western Europe, Stalin watched every move carefully. The rapid German victory in France did not please him at all, for he knew that Hitler, if easily victorious in the west, might attack Russia. On the other hand, everyone saw that if England and France and Germany bled each other white, then Soviet Russia would be able to spread her power farther and farther. That is what Josef Stalin and the Communists are counting on—that more and more of the countries of Europe and Asia will become Socialist states under Russian influence. Only time can tell whether they are right or wrong.

Hitler

Hitler Challenges the West

O NE of Adolf Hitler's heroes is Frederick the Great. This is not surprising, for Frederick tried to do in Prussia what Hitler is trying to do in Germany. There is another similarity, too. Frederick feared and hated his father. And Adolf Hitler, when he was a boy, regarded his father with anything but devotion.

The older Hitler, a minor customs official for the Austrian government, was a dissatisfied, harsh man, who drank heavily, to try to forget that he was poor and unsuccessful. He was married three times. His first two wives died, after bearing him several children. Then he married Adolf's mother. Young Adolf grew up in a small Austrian town, living in a house where there was little pleasure. His mother, whom he loved, was sick much of the time; and his father would often storm and stamp around the rooms, cursing and even beating members of the family who angered him.

A DREAM OF WAR

Like all boys, Adolf used to day-dream about what a great man he would be when he grew up. His favorite dream was that he was a general, leading an army to war. But not the Austrian army. He knew that Austria was not a very strong country, and that Germany had the best soldiers in Europe. In his day-dreams he was always the commander of a German army. Among his father's books were some which told how Germany had beaten France in Bismarck's time. Adolf used to read these books all the time, and think of himself in a German uniform, leading his men to victory against France.

The fact that he was an Austrian did not trouble him. For he told himself that Austrians, too, were really Germans, and that the two countries belonged together.

This day-dream may sound like that of any other child, but actually it has played an important part in history. For when Adolf Hitler grew up, he continued to believe that Austria should belong to Germany. It seemed to him that all people who had German ancestors were really part of the German nation, no matter what country they lived in—even if they were citizens of Poland, or Denmark, or France, or the United States. And this idea helped him greatly in his rise to power, which has had such tremendous results for Germany and the world.

ADOLF STUDIES ART

As he grew older, and learned a little more about life, he realized that he would have to forget about being a general, and prepare for some less dreamlike career. But the ordinary trades and professions did not appeal to him. They were not exciting enough. His father cursed him for being lazy, but he was not really lazy; he was romantic.

Finally he decided what he wanted to be—an artist! At school he had found that he could draw better than most of his fellow-students. And the artist's life, as he had read about it in books, seemed full of romance and fun.

His mother, who loved him as tenderly as he loved her, encouraged him. Finally Adolf summoned up courage enough to ask his father to send him to an art school. Hitler senior raged at the idea. It only proved, he shouted, that Adolf wanted to avoid real work. He made his son go instead to a "practical school."

Adolf hated the school. When his father died, he was really glad. His ailing mother had a little money, and she gave Adolf enough to send him to art school at last. These, he himself has said, were his "happiest days."

But two years later his mother, too, died. Adolf now had only a tiny sum of money. Still, he was determined to be an artist. He journeyed to Vienna, where there was a great Academy of Art, hoping to continue his studies there.

But before the Academy would allow him to enter, he had to take an examination—and he failed. He was heartbroken. He thought perhaps he might become an architect. The architects' school, however, also refused to admit him.

Adolf was filled with bitterness. He envied the luckier boys who were allowed to enter the Academy and the technical school. Some of these boys were Jewish, and Adolf particularly resented them. Why should they be accepted, while he was refused? It did not occur to him that the boys who got into the Academy might have had more talent than he. He began to hate the Jews. Of course, he knew practically nothing about the Jewish race and its history, or the great part it has played in building civilization.

HATRED

He had to find work in a hurry, and he became assistant to a house painter. It was a painful come-down for a young man who had dreamed of fame in war and art. He lived in a cheap room, ate cheap food, wore cheap clothes, had no money for amusements. Around him, in the streets of Vienna, he saw wealthy men, wearing furs and silks, riding in carriages with beautiful women, going to theaters and glittering restaurants and cafés. Some of these lucky people too were Jews. Adolf bit his lips. How unfair that Jews should have these privileges, he thought, while he, a German of "pure blood," had to go on slapping paint on walls, day after day, for long hours.

Other poor young men in similar circumstances—like Benito Mussolini and Josef Stalin—joined labor unions. They became Socialists, in order—so they thought—to work for a government under which poor people might have more pleasure in life. But Hitler did not like labor unions. All this talk about wages and hours and strikes seemed petty, compared with his wonderful dreams. He did not care about the rights of the working class. What he wanted was the rights of Adolf Hitler—the right to be famous and admired. Besides, there were some Jews in the labor unions and in the Socialist party, and by this time he would have nothing to do with Jews.

Finally he could no longer stand his work as a laborer. He decided to go hungry if necessary, but to be an artist. At the age of twenty-one, in 1910, he left Vienna and went to Munich, in Germany, where he became a painter of cheap watercolor pictures.

"I believe," he has written, "that those who knew me then thought me a queer chap."

But this life was unsatisfactory, too. People did not want his paintings. Other artists shrugged their shoulders. They said his work was old-fashioned and lacked imagination. Hitler was furious, and began to hate the modern artists as much as he hated Jews and Socialists. Years were passing; and the world simply would not admit that he was a great man.

In his spare time he read books. But as he himself has related, he never read books which contradicted his ideas, and which might have taught him something, because they made him uncomfortable. He preferred books which attacked the Jews, or which told about the wonderful German nation.

THE "ARYAN RACE"

In particular the lives of Frederick the Great and Bismarck appealed to him. And a certain book by a Frenchman, which described the "Aryan race," made a deep impression on him. According to this book, which nowadays would be laughed at, the "Aryans" were a race of conquerors, who swept over central and western Europe many centuries ago. Hitler seized upon this notion. The Germans, he decided, were "pure Aryans"—a "master race"—and all other races were inferior. This made him feel good, because he, of course, was a German.

Scientists know that no "Aryan race" ever existed. But Hitler never read the books of scientists. He preferred his dreams. If he had studied the question, he would have learned that the word "Aryan" describes not a race, but a number of languages with a common origin, and that these languages are spoken by people of many different types. And he would have found out that there is no such thing as a "pure race," in Germany or anywhere else. In the course of time the races of Europe have mingled so much that every country is connected by "blood" with every other country. As you will remember, in Frederick the Great's day a large number of Prussians were immigrants from Poland and Bohemia.

Hitler, however, preferred his own ideas. He was sure there was a conquering "Aryan race" in Germany, and he was part of it. To use his own words, "Germany must some day be master of the world."

All of us like to regard our nation and our race as "the best," of course. To love and respect one's own country is natural and healthy. But as men and women become better educated, they realize that there is not very much difference, after all, between one civilized people and any other. In fact, it is the uncivilized peoples who are most certain that they are superior. For example, an American Indian tribe called itself the Kiowa, which means "the only real people." A South American tribe has a saying, "We alone are people." In Greenland, when the Eskimos want to praise a European or an American, they say that he will soon be as good as an Eskimo. Several thousand years ago the primitive Jews were sure that they were "The Chosen."

Modern civilized peoples have been getting away from these absurd notions that one tribe or one nation is so much better than any other. Americans, Germans, Spanish, French, English, Czechs, Italians, Swedes, Russians, Chinese, Japanese, all have their virtues and their failings. Hitler did not realize that in asserting that the Germans were the *only* race fitted to rule he was going back thousands of years to the selfishness and hatreds of savage tribes.

THE NEW DREAM AND THE WAR

As these notions grew in his mind, he saw himself as the hero of a new day-dream. He decided that the pure German race was being held back by the Jews and the Socialist labor unions. Soon a hero would come who would destroy the Jews and Socialists, and lead the Germans to their "true destiny" as the conquerors of the world.

Hitler was very fond of Richard Wagner's operas, which tell how the hero Siegfried rescues the beautiful Brünhilde from an enchanted sleep. He saw himself as the Siegfried of the German people.

Then, in 1914, the first World War broke out. He had to forget his dream for a while, and become a private in the German army, on the western front. For a while he was enthusiastic about the war. But soon, as he has said, "The romance of the battles turned to horror." Nevertheless, he fought bravely, and was wounded.

When Germany lost, he was crushed. How could a race of conquerors be defeated? But he quickly found an explanation. Of course! The Jews and the German Socialists had defeated his country by working against the army from behind the ranks!

THE TROUBLES OF GERMANY

The truth was that both the German army and the German people were hungry, miserable, and sick of the war; while France and England were being helped by millions of American soldiers and billions of American dollars. When the war ended, the Germans were bitter. They knew that the war had been made by the men who owned and governed their country, as well as the other countries of Europe. They were of a mind to deal with their aristocrats and wealthy men as the Russians had done two years before.

Angry mobs began to gather in Berlin. Kaiser William II gave up his throne and fled to Holland. For a while it looked as if Germany too were about to have a Socialist revolution, for the Socialists were the biggest party in the country.

But the victorious Allied governments had no desire to see Germany become socialistic, lest her example be followed in France and England and Italy, where the people were also bitter at having had to endure so much suffering. The Allies sent troops into Germany to prevent the Socialists from taking power. A republic was set up, with a President and ministers who agreed not to disturb the property of the big landowners and business men.

The powerful Communist section of the Socialists was, of course, very dissatisfied with this arrangement. The Communists kept urging ex-soldiers to revolt against the republic, and make all land and factories the property of the people as a whole, to be run by the government. But the German people are accustomed to obey their government, whether they like it or not, and after some fighting, the Communist revolt failed.

The Allies kept their troops in Germany until the people had quieted down, and then turned the job of policing the country over to the new German army, called the Reichswehr. This was a small force, of only about 100,000 men—all that was permitted by the treaty of Versailles. But the men were picked men, and the army had excellent guns, so that it was stronger than one would guess from the mere numbers.

In 1919 Hitler joined the Reichswehr, and was made a corporal, stationed at Munich. One day his officers assigned him to special duty. He was to go out among the people, especially among the laborers, and listen to what they were saying, and report back to headquarters. For there was still talk of revolution in many groups, and the aristocrats who led the Reichswehr wanted to know where "the trouble makers" were. Hitler was a sort of spy.

THE BEGINNINGS OF THE NAZIS

There was a small group of half a dozen men in Munich who called themselves the German Workers' party, and who were suspected of being revolutionists. Hitler was told to see what they were up to. He attended one of their meetings, heard some speeches, and found that these men had some ideas that he agreed with. He was so excited that he joined the party, becoming member number 7. And this was the beginning of the great Nazi movement.

Hitler, too, made some speeches, and discovered that he was a very powerful orator, who could hold an audience spellbound. In fact, he was never so happy as when he was on a platform, shouting himself hoarse. He could make himself believe anything he said, even if it was nonsense; and his sincerity and passion impressed almost everybody who heard him. He had no hesitation about telling lies if it would help his cause. He wrote, "The people have no idea how they must be misled." By the middle of 1920, when his term of service in the Reichswehr was finished, he was the leader of the German Workers' party, small as it was, and he began to devote all his time to politics.

The only ideas that he really cared about were the same old ones. Germany had to become the greatest nation in the world, a conquering nation. The Jews had to be destroyed. And the new republic, with its Reichstag, also had to be abolished, because it was full of Liberals and Social-Democrats and Communists, all of whom Hitler despised. His idea was to have a dictatorship without political parties.

But he knew that these aims alone were not enough to make workmen join his new party. For the workmen were interested in things like how much money they could earn, and how many hours a day they had to work. So Hitler added a number of other ideas to his program—ideas which he borrowed from the Socialists and Communists.

He said that nobody should be allowed to get interest on money—which meant that banks and wealthy people who owned bonds and stocks would be ruined. He said that business men who had made profits during the war should be forced to give them up to the government, and that all big businesses should be owned by the people and managed by the government. He said that the big landed estates should be taken away from the aristocrats and divided up among the poor peasants. In fact, he sounded in some respects very much like a Communist.

HITLER'S INFLUENCE GROWS

As you will remember, about this time Mussolini, in Italy, was building up his Fascist party, and saying almost exactly the same

things, except that he had nothing against the Jews. Like Mussolini, Hitler did not really care very much one way or the other
who owned the factories and land, so long as he could be important, and smash the Reichstag and the Jews, and lead Germany to victory. He knew his best chance of becoming important
was to pretend to be on the side of the workmen. For this reason
he changed the name of his party to "National Socialist German
Workers party"—which the world has shortened to "the Nazis."
By means of this name and his radical program he hoped to get
the workmen to desert the real Socialists and join with him.
Then the aristocrats and the big business men would have to
pay attention to him.

His reputation as a speaker began to spread, and more and
more people came to the party meetings to hear him. He began
in 1919 by addressing audiences of twenty. In 1920, he was speaking to 2000 at a time, and in 1921 to crowds of 6000.

People were fascinated by him, especially the young unemployed ex-soldiers. They were miserable, and wanted somebody
to blame for their misery, and when he told them to blame the
Jews and the Communists, they were entirely willing. They
were patriotic, and wanted a dream of glory, and when he told
them his dream of Germany's "destiny" as master of the world,
they cheered and shouted.

Money began to come in from supporters. Some say that
wealthy Americans who disliked labor unions and Jews con-
tributed to Hitler's treasury. He was able to start a newspaper,
and to buy uniforms for his followers—brown shirts, instead of
black shirts as in Italy. Like Mussolini again, he formed his men
into bands, and they attacked meetings of Communists and
striking workmen, and beat up their opponents with clubs and

fists. In 1922, after Mussolini's *Fascisti* marched on Rome, the eyes of the world turned to Hitler. Would he, too, destroy democracy in his country?

THE FIRST ATTEMPT FAILS

Some aristocratic German army officers were also backing Hitler. In 1923 they encouraged him to revolt openly against the republic. He and a number of his followers met in a Munich beer hall, and then dashed out into the street to fight the police and seize the government buildings—hoping that the revolt would thereafter spread all over Germany.

But the people failed to come to his aid, and the police resisted. After an exchange of shots, the Nazis fled. Hitler's reputation for bravery suffered, because he fell flat on his face while the shooting was going on, and stayed there until it was over. Some people say, however, that he was pulled down by another Nazi. Whatever the truth may be, he tried to get away in a motor car, but was soon arrested.

A court convicted him of treason and sentenced him to prison for five years. Most people thought that the failure of the "beer hall revolt" meant the end of his career. But he was still confident. While in jail he wrote a book—the famous *Mein Kampf,* or *My Battle*. In this long and passionate book he told the story of his life, and his ideas about government.

Parts of the book show that Hitler has a shrewd, practical mind and a deep understanding of the way people think. But there are other parts which are full of outright lies and absolute nonsense. For Hitler knows that millions of people will believe lies and nonsense if they are repeated over and over.

Today *Mein Kampf* is the bible of Germany, and millions of Germans would be willing to kill anybody who says that there are lies in the book. Yet Hitler himself has admitted that he has often lied "because it was necessary"—meaning that was the only way in which he could come to power.

His aristocratic friends were quietly working for him behind the scenes. They urged the politicians of the republic to let Hitler out of jail, and after eight months the government pardoned him. Once more he began to address overflowing meetings all over Germany.

THE ALLIES HELP HITLER

Now the Nazi party began to grow faster than ever before— by the millions. For while Hitler was in prison, the world had unconsciously been helping his cause. Just how this had happened is a somewhat complicated story; but international politics is always complicated. To grasp the meaning of historical events you must look beneath the surface.

When the Versailles peace treaty was made in 1919, all the blame for beginning the war was put on Germany. This was not fair, since England and France certainly were partly responsible. However, Germany was forced to pay the Allied countries a tremendous sum of money—many billions of dollars—which was called "reparations" for damage done in the war.

The only way the German government could get this money was by borrowing it. But this was not easy. During the war the German people had lent almost everything they had to the Kaiser's government. They had bought government bonds to pay for guns and airplanes. They had nothing left to lend to the republic.

The republican government then tried to borrow the money it needed from the big bankers of New York and London and Paris. At first the bankers said, "It would not be good business to lend you this money while you already owe so much to your own people."

Then the German politicians said that if they did not get money somehow, their government would fail, and the Communists would seize power. The other countries did not like this idea at all, because they were afraid of the Communists. Finally they hinted to the desperate German government, "If there was some way you could wipe out the debt you owe to your own people, we would lend you the money you need."

THE PEOPLE ARE TRICKED

The German government then wiped out its debt to the German people by what is known as "inflation of the currency." They printed a vast amount of paper money. And they said to the people who owned government bonds, "The German government owes you a million marks. Very well, here is paper money printed in the amount of a million marks. Don't blame us if it isn't worth anything. We're doing the best we can." (A mark had once been worth about twenty-five American cents in gold, so that a person who held bonds for a million marks might have lent the government $250,000.)

Have you ever stopped to think why the printed pieces of paper that we call money are valuable? Usually it is because people have faith that their government will, if asked, exchange the paper for gold, or silver, or some other valuable thing. In Germany, at the time we are speaking about, nobody had such faith.

For there was very little gold and silver in the treasury, and the government was printing billions and billions of paper marks.

As soon as the German people realized what was happening, paper money lost all its value. A man might have ten million paper marks in his pocket and yet be unable to buy a cup of coffee. Millions of Germans who had lent their money to the government received meaningless pieces of paper in return. They were ruined.

Having wiped out the debt to German bondholders, the German government was able to borrow a large sum from some big Wall Street bankers. Then the government got rid of all its worthless money, and issued some new money in which people had faith, and which could be used to buy things.

The German politicians were well pleased, because they were able to keep their power over the German government, and to prevent the Communists from becoming too strong for them. But many of the German people felt that they had been tricked and cheated out of their money, and they hated the politicians and the republican government.

HITLER TAKES ADVANTAGE

It is easy to see how all this helped Adolf Hitler. He made speech after speech attacking the German republican politicians and the international bankers for the inflation. He said, falsely, that the bankers were all Jews, and promised to avenge the German people by destroying the German Jews and the politicians.

Of course, he hated the Communists, too, which mixed things up; for the bankers and republican politicians and many Jewish business men were also fighting the Communists. In fact, some

Jewish business men disliked the Communists so much that they actually supported Hitler, for they thought he did not mean what he said about the Jews. It seemed ridiculous that anyone could seriously blame the Jews for Germany's troubles. For of sixty million Germans, only one out of a hundred had any Jewish blood, and most of these were no better off than anyone else.

But in Berlin and a few other cities there were a good many prosperous Jewish business men, lawyers, and doctors. It was easy for Hitler to make poor Germans envious of these lucky ones. In this way he was able to work up feeling against all Jews.

Many Germans were so eager to hate somebody and to get revenge for their suffering, that they cheered when Hitler raved against Jews and politicians and foreign bankers and Communists all together. They did not mind being confused, because Hitler was so exciting.

In fact, one of the strongest reasons for Hitler's success is that he did not ask his followers to think. He said, "Trust me, and all will be well." And they did. They put their faith in him blindly, because then they did not have to figure things out for themselves. They said, "Our great leader Adolf Hitler will do our thinking for us. All we have to do is obey." In every country, including our own, there are many people with lazy minds who like to follow a leader blindly, like sheep. Between 1923 and 1932, millions of Germans flocked to join the Nazis.

As hard times continued in Germany, the Socialist parties and the labor unions were also growing. Some big business men were particularly alarmed by the strength of the Communists. They decided that Hitler was their best hope for fighting the Communists. They turned to him just as Italian conservatives had turned to Mussolini. They promised to help Hitler come to power, if he would break up the German labor unions, and let the big landowners keep their land and pay lower taxes.

Like the Italian leader, Hitler was willing to make any kind of deal in order to come to power. He threw overboard the old program of his party, with its socialistic ideas. He came out frankly against the labor unions. He said that workmen should have nothing to say about wages and hours, and had no claim to share in property.

This pleased the German conservatives, but it upset some of the older members of the Nazi party, who were still on the side of the workmen. Hitler made these discontented Nazis get out of the party. Then some of the wealthy men gave him money to help build up the Nazi party. And in 1933 they tricked the aged President of the republic, Hindenburg, into appointing Hitler as Prime Minister, or Chancellor.

THE NAZIS START A FIRE

According to the law of the republic, before Hitler could take office as Chancellor, a new Reichstag, or parliament, would have to be elected and give its approval. Hitler and his two chief assistants, Göring and Goebbels, were afraid that the German people would not give the Nazis a big enough vote in the elections. They feared that the Reichstag would oppose Hitler and weaken his power. So they planned a scheme that was even more startling than the one that Napoleon and Sieyès used to overthrow the French parliament.

One night the great hall of the Reichstag burst into flame. Hitler cried that the fire had been started by the Communists and was proof of a Communist plot to revolt against the government.

He issued a decree, arresting 4000 leading Communists. He shut down Communist and Socialist newspapers. He forbade meetings of Socialists. He announced that a great conspiracy to destroy the country had been uncovered in the nick of time.

All this frightened the nation so much that when the elections were held, the Nazis received nearly half of all the votes cast. This was enough to give Hitler control of the Reichstag.

Of course, the great "conspiracy" turned out to be a fairy tale. The Nazis held a trial of some accused Communists, but even their own judges could not find that the Communists had anything to do with the fire. Soon all the world realized that the Nazis themselves had deliberately burned down the Reichstag in order to make sure that Hitler would win the elections, and give him an excuse for smashing the Communist party.

THE NAZIS TAKE POWER

Everything went as Hitler had planned.

The Reichstag voted to make him dictator. When old Hindenburg died, the office of President was abolished. The army took an oath of allegiance to Adolf Hitler, Leader and Chancellor of the Reich.

The labor unions were dissolved, and their money, saved up by the workmen, was taken away. The factory workmen were forced to obey the Nazis. Wages began to fall, and hours of work to grow.

All political parties except the Nazis were disbanded and forbidden to hold meetings. Nothing could be printed or shown in a motion picture, or spoken on the radio, unless the Nazis approved.

Jews all over Germany were beaten up and killed. Their property and businesses were taken away and given to Nazi business men. It soon became impossible for many Jews to live, and they starved to death, or committed suicide.

Scientists, writers, and artists who opposed Hitler, including many of the country's most famous men, fled from Germany for their lives. Those who did not get out in time went to prison. When Göring, one of the Nazi leaders, heard complaints of injustice, he said, "My business is not to do justice, but to destroy."

A great secret police force, the *Gestapo,* began to search out every man suspected of being against Hitler, and put the victims into "concentration camps." Liberals, Socialists, Jews, and even Nazis filled these concentration camps by the hundreds of thousands. Many of them were systematically beaten and tortured by Nazi troopers until their spirit was broken. Thousands were killed and crippled. Others went mad.

THE BLOOD PURGE

A year after taking power, Hitler realized that a great many Nazi Stormtroopers were not satisfied with the way things were going. Hitler had once promised them to take businesses away not only from the Jews but from Christian business men as well, and to give these businesses to the Nazis. But now he feared that the business men and the army would revolt if he tried it.

He did not dare tell the dissatisfied Nazis that he was not going to keep his promise to them because that too might have caused a revolt. But he had to do something, particularly as one of his best friends, Captain Röhm, was the leader of these "radicals" in the party, and kept asking him what his intentions were.

One day in June 1934 Hitler sent cordial telegrams to Röhm and to hundreds of the other leaders of the radical Nazis, asking them to meet him in a certain city. As they got off the trains, they were amazed to find thousands of Hitler's private guards waiting to arrest them. Without any warning or any chance to speak they were led to a fortress. Twenty of them, pale and bewildered at this treachery, were forced to stand up against a wall. A platoon of soldiers leveled their rifles. The commanding officer cried, "This is done at the wish of the leader. Heil Hitler! Fire!"

A volley rang out, and the betrayed Nazis fell. Another score were stood up against the wall. Another volley. And another and another until there were hundreds of dead bodies lying there. Some of the unfortunate men, who had only been wounded by the bullets, were finished off with blows on the head.

Hitler did not want to have it said that he had ordered his dear friend Röhm to be killed. So he gave instructions to have Röhm put in a cell, with a pistol. However, Röhm refused to commit suicide. When he heard the shots from outside, he smiled grimly and said, "If Adolf wants me to be shot, he will have to do it himself." Finally, he too was taken out and shot.

Thus Hitler made himself secure—on the dead bodies of his own "Aryan brothers in arms."

During this "blood purge" of the Nazis, Hitler also sent a squad of soldiers to the home of a certain famous aristocratic General, named von Schleicher, who was respected by most of the Germans, and whom Hitler feared. The Nazis forced their way into the General's house, without warning fired a dozen shots into him, mortally wounded his wife, and left them lying on the doorstep of their home.

HITLER'S AGENTS GO TO WORK IN AMERICA

Then Hitler sent out secret agents to all important countries, including the United States. These agents began to organize branches of the Nazi party. In America they persuaded many people of German blood to form "Bunds," where they marched and drilled in the German manner, and promised to "fight for the fatherland," meaning Germany.

Hitler's agents also tried to win some American conservatives to their side by promising to help smash the American labor unions and Socialists. They worked together with some Americans who wanted to imitate Hitler. They helped to start various parties and groups which want to do in this country what Hitler has done in Germany.

All these groups have one thing in common: they attack American citizens of Jewish origin. For in America, too, there are many poor and miserable people who would like to blame someone for their sufferings. The Nazis and American Fascists tell these unfortunates that the Jews are to blame, and that once the Jews are destroyed, everything will be fine. Luckily, not many Americans are foolish enough to be taken in by this nonsense. Most of us know that the real purpose of the American Nazis is to set up a rule of violence which will give the power and wealth of the country to them, and which will force the workmen and small farmers of America to work for starvation wages, as they do in Germany.

HITLER THRILLS GERMANY

Although German workmen and peasants had to work harder and for less money than before—although they were really becoming slaves to the Nazis and to the army—they soon began to think that Hitler was wonderful. Life in Germany was exciting. All Germans were full of new courage. They were proud of being German and "Aryan." Everywhere there was a feeling of hope and a great love for *der Führer,* the leader.

The children in the schools learned to sing songs in Hitler's praise. The boys and young men formed in groups called "Hitler Youth," and they marched and cheered and sang for Hitler. In outdoor labor camps lusty young men hardened their muscles with ax and shovel, and sang the Nazi songs. The factory workers were sent on holidays by the Nazis, and they too cheered for the wonderful Adolf. The Nazi party held great meetings in the open air, at which millions of men and women wept with happiness at the magic words of their leader. As for the business men and aristocrats, they too spoke of Hitler with pleasure, for they were making more money than before.

Just as he had promised, Hitler had united Germany behind him. He was leading Germany to her rightful place among the nations. He had put an end to the hated Versailles treaty. He had withdrawn Germany from the League of Nations, which was run by France and England. He was rapidly building up the German army and air force. He was building a great line of forts at the French border. By 1936 he was openly helping the Spanish Fascists win the civil war in Spain, and was thumbing his nose at the French protests.

And all Germany knew that these tremendous deeds were only a beginning.

Nevertheless, there was some opposition to Hitler. Much of it came from the Catholic and Protestant Churches in Germany. The priests and pastors refused to change the Christian religion to suit Hitler. They continued to teach that mercy and love and peace were good things.

Hitler was furious at this disobedience. The Nazis wanted the Churches to teach that war was good, and that Christ was a German, and that mercy and peace were "un-German ideas." They said that the Christian idea of loving one's neighbor was foolish, and that the only thing that mattered was the power of Germany. They even tried to set up a new religion of their own, which revived the worship of the old pagan war gods, Wotan and Thor.

Finally Hitler put a number of pastors of the Protestant Church in prison, and began to close churches right and left. With the Catholic Church, however, he was more cautious. For he remembered Bismarck's defeat by the Church. He signed a kind of treaty with the Pope, and promised to respect the rights and property of the Church.

Nevertheless, Hitler bullied the liberal Catholic leaders. One Cardinal had to fly for his life from Nazi mobs. And Hitler also destroyed the influence of the Church in educating the youth of the country.

HITLER BEGINS TO CONQUER

As 1937 went by, even Germans who were not religious became a little dissatisfied. Wages kept going down. Taxes kept going up. The army was getting all the money of the country. Most people were not eating enough meat, or eggs, or white bread, or butter. More than half of the families of the country could not get along on their wages, and had to be given "relief" by the government.

Hitler knew that people are changeable, and that unless he revived the spirit of the country, the Germans would lose their faith in him. Like Mussolini, he saw that the time had come to make the people cheer. And the best way of making them cheer was by conquering some other country.

Austria was afraid of his intentions, so the Austrians asked him to sign a treaty saying that he recognized their independence. He signed it with his tongue in his cheek. A month later he suddenly sent his army into Austria, and captured the country overnight. The little Austrian army made no attempt to resist. In this way, the dream of his boyhood became a fact. Austria and Germany were one at last.

The German people were excited and pleased. As for the conservative governments of England and France, they did not care very much. They said, "After all, the Austrians are really Germans."

England and France were worried, however, about Czecho-Slovakia. For they had a treaty with the Czechs, and had promised to defend them against an attack by Germany. They asked Germany to agree to let Czecho-Slovakia alone, and the Nazis agreed. Göring gave his "word of honor" that Germany would not bother the Czechs.

In the northern part of Czecho-Slovakia, called the Sudetenland, lived a good many Germans. They had always got along pretty well with the Czechs. Then Hitler sent his agents among them to make them revolt. Soon the Sudeten Nazis were demanding that the Sudetenland be made a part of Germany.

Hitler said that he would free these "pure" Germans from "the brutal Czechs." He sent his army to the border and threatened to invade Czecho-Slovakia at once. The Czechs, who are a brave people, prepared to defend themselves, and asked England and France to keep their promise to help.

But the conservative English and French governments still wanted to avoid war. They said, "After all, the people in the Sudetenland are Germans, too." And they said, "What if we have made a promise to the Czechs? Promises do not matter much in politics."

The English Prime Minister Chamberlain and the French Prime Minister Daladier went to Germany to talk things over with Hitler and Mussolini. They said that Hitler could take the Sudetenland, if he would leave the rest of Czecho-Slovakia alone.

The Czechs saw that they could not fight Germany by themselves, so they had to give in. Hitler sent his army into the Sudetenland. And the German people, who had begun to worry about a serious war, went wild with happiness.

Of course, liberals and Socialists and Jews in Austria and the Sudetenland were at once driven out of business, and beaten, and sent to concentration camps, or killed. But the world was becoming used to that kind of thing now. No one objected very much.

CZECHO-SLOVAKIA FALLS

Now Hitler said he was satisfied. He told France and England, "The Sudetenland is the last territory that I want in Europe." A few months later his army marched into Czecho-Slovakia and occupied the whole country. England and France protested, and said it was a shame, while the Germans and Italians laughed at them.

Since the Czechs and the Slovaks are not Germans, some people could not understand why Hitler wanted them in Germany —especially since he was always talking about a "pure German race." But the fact is he did not care about the Czechs and Slovaks. He wanted their factories and farms and money, and he took a great deal of their property away from them, and gave it to Germans.

Liberals and Socialists and Jews were again destroyed. The rest of the Czechs soon found that they were becoming slaves to the Nazis. They had to work and pay, and work and pay, in order to make the German army stronger and stronger. Some of them tried to rebel, and were shot down in the streets.

As soon as Czecho-Slovakia had been conquered, Hitler turned his attention to Poland.

ALARM IN THE WEST

England and France finally saw that unless they stopped Hitler, he would conquer all central Europe. That would make him so strong that he could probably defeat them in a war, and take away all their valuable colonies. The English and French conservatives who had approved of Hitler when he broke up the German labor unions, now began to fear him, because he was beginning to threaten their own possessions.

So England and France hurriedly began to build up their own armies and air forces. They warned Hitler that if he attempted to conquer any other countries in Europe they would fight—and this time they meant it.

Hitler did not believe they meant it. He decided that the English and French, with their "democracy," were soft, and that he could do what he wished in central Europe. Besides, he was more afraid of peace than of war. The German army was costing so much that the rest of the people were getting less and less to eat every week. Like Mussolini, Hitler knew that the people would put up with suffering only if they thought it was in a good cause.

He told them that the Poles were mistreating some Germans who lived in Poland, and whipped up the anger of the German people against Poland. Then he made his deal with Stalin, to be sure that the Russian army would not help the Poles. After that he told the Nazis to march. In a few weeks, he had conquered Poland, and had taken half of the country for Germany, while the other half went to Russia. Thereafter he seized Denmark and most of Norway

THE WAR NOBODY WANTED

Meanwhile, the British and French unwillingly went to war against Germany. The English fleet blockaded Germany, and English and French troops helped the Norwegians resist. They hoped to starve Germany into surrender. But the German submarines and airplanes sank a great many British merchant ships, and fought with the Allied warships and air forces. Then Hitler sent his famous armored columns crashing into Holland and Belgium, and the "Total War" broke out in northern France— the war to the death that Hitler had long threatened. London and Paris prepared to defend themselves. And the whole world watched with bated breath as the greatest battles ever seen destroyed lives by the hundreds of thousands. France fell. England fought on.

As to whether Germany or England will win the war—that depends largely on which peoples have the most fighting spirit and determination to win. For in a war where both sides have great military power, it is usually the spirit of the people at home which decides the victory.

The English are famous for their fighting spirit. But so are the Germans. You need only remember how well the Prussians fought for Frederick the Great in the Seven Years' War to realize that they will not give in easily.

However, in this war the Germans are fighting under a handicap. Germany does not grow enough food to feed all the Germans. She has no oil wells of her own, and oil is needed to run airplanes, railroads, and submarines.

For years the Nazis have been buying food and oil abroad and storing it up, knowing that sooner or later there would be a war. But these supplies will not last long. The Germans must keep on buying from neutral countries which have an extra supply of food and oil.

Since the British fleet will not allow ships to bring wheat and oil to Germany, the Germans have to import these things by land —from Russia and the Balkans—or by the Baltic Sea, from Scandinavia. And they do not have much money or extra goods with which to pay the other countries. Many people think that to win this war, Germany will have to conquer some Balkan peoples and the Swedes, too, and take their wheat and oil and other goods away from them.

INTO THE FUTURE

Thus the world finds itself once more engaged in a horrible struggle, with millions of decent men and women having to suffer hunger, and wounds, and death. Why? This is a difficult question. The trouble seems to arise largely from man's selfishness and fear—for selfishness and fear go together. Selfish business men and selfish labor unions fear and fight each other. Selfish political parties fear and hate each other. Selfish leaders try to gain power for themselves. And presently the peoples of the nations are so distressed and bewildered that they too become fearful and greedy, and try to destroy each other.

Perhaps some day the peoples of the world will learn to settle their differences by peaceful methods. Certainly that day is far distant—hardly more than a dream. But dreams have power, both for good and for evil. You have seen how the boyhood dream of Adolf Hitler came true. If enough people share the dream of a world in which the leaders of nations work to avoid war instead of to make it, then that dream too may also in time turn into reality.

Postscript

◆◇◆

About Power and Democracy

WHAT is this wonderful thing called power, for which some men, as you have seen, will cheat, rob, bribe, starve, and kill thousands of their fellow-men?

In politics, power is the ability of one man to make others do what he wishes.

Suppose people refuse to do what the man of power wishes? Then his power is gone. It is the people who confer power on a ruler.

But once a people has given power to a dictator, it is hard for them to disobey him. Before they can do so, they must be able to fight his police and soldiers.

So that even if a dictator is ruining and starving his people, they may not be able to take back the power that they have given him.

That is why we in America value democracy so highly.

Democracy is a way to make sure that if our leaders abuse the power which we, the people, lend them, we can take it away from them without having to fight police and soldiers.

True, if we are forced to defend ourselves in a war against dangerous enemies, then in order to win we may have to give up some of our democratic privileges for a while. Nations fight best when there is a single trusted leader in complete control. But in that case we must try to select an honest man to lead us, one who himself respects democracy and who does not aspire to be a Napoleon or a Hitler. We must do everything possible to make sure that as soon as the emergency is over, our democratic rights are returned to us.

In these perilous times, it is more important than ever to remember the powers which democracy gives to us, the people.

It allows all of us who are law-abiding to vote in elections, in which a poor man's vote counts for as much as a rich man's. We do not have to tell anybody how we are voting unless we choose to. And whatever most of us vote for, that is what we get.

Nobody can force us to vote for anybody we do not like. We have a choice of candidates at every election, representing different political points of view.

If we find that a President, or Senator, or Governor, or Mayor, or any other public official is using his power selfishly, to benefit himself and a few supporters at the expense of the people as a whole—if that happens, we can vote against him at the next election, and throw him out of office. Or if we do not wish to wait that long, we can appeal to the courts of our nation to protect us.

Every one of us has the right of free speech. We can say what we please about our government and our laws.

The press is free. We have the right to print our opinions and get other people to read them.

Everybody can worship according to his own religion. Race and color of skin make no difference to our rights as citizens.

All these rights go with democracy. But democracy is more than a series of political privileges, great as they may be.

Democracy is a way of living. Deep-rooted in it are the ideas of fair play, and of tolerance. Out of democracy, too, grows the precious feeling that each of us, no matter what his station in life, is entitled to the respect of his fellows—respect as a human being.

Today the world is changing about us. As time goes on, many of the laws of our country will have to change to suit the new conditions which arise. Under democracy, if we are wise, we can bring about whatever changes prove necessary without bloodshed and violence.

To be sure, democracy works slowly and often clumsily. But in the long run it works with far less pain than dictatorship, with its "blood purges," its slavery, its revolutions, and its needless wars.

It is not enough merely to be proud of our democracy, and to believe in it. Some clever, selfish, ambitious men, would-be Hitlers and Mussolinis and Stalins, would gladly take it away from us if they could. If we are to keep our democracy intact and make it even stronger, then we must know how to protect it against these men.

We must be on our guard to see through the lies and empty promises with which men of power often trick people into giving up their rights.

We must avoid the unnecessary wars into which men of power sometimes force peoples, in order to gain supreme control; for war and powerful armies have often been the means of destroying democracy.

We must make sure that the peacetime law-making powers of our Congress, elected by our votes, are not taken away, either by force or by trickery.

If we work hard enough to preserve democracy, if we do not get lazy and careless about it, no one will be able to take it away from us.

We Americans need no men of power. Even when the absolute ruler has good intentions, power usually runs away with him, and forces him into crushing millions of his countrymen.

The chief value of the man of power to ordinary people is that he makes life exciting. But, as we know, the people in a dictatorship pay a high and a terrible price for their excitement. We in America do not need or want excitement at that price. We can get our thrill by reading about the dictators of less fortunate countries. Or better still, we can thrill to these grand words:

We hold these truths to be self-evident: That all men are created equal; that they are endowed by their Creator with certain inalienable rights; that among these are life, liberty, and the pursuit of happiness; that, to secure these rights, governments are instituted among men, deriving their just powers from the consent of the governed.

—From the DECLARATION OF INDEPENDENCE

And the last point which we must consider is the codes
of ethics themselves which were evolved by our two subjects.
Plato is rather vague on this point, of the actual mechanics
of ethics, but he does say flatly in the Philebus that the
ideal life at which our ethics must aim is a mixture of intelligence and pleasure, with intelligence in the majority. He goes
on to affirm that the life of wisdom, while not complete in itself
is probably the highest man ifestation of the human mind. He
tells us that "Pleasure is not akin to the good, because it is in-
herently boundless, unlimited, insatiate.   Intelligence is akin
to the good, because it is akin to the principle of limit."
because it is everywhere a principle of cause ad

Never in the obvious way that Aristotle flatly states it,
but nevertheless present, is the ancinet famed and defam ed Gre-
cian idea of the Golden Mean, of Nothing over mcun.

Aristotle seems to have three main ideas in his concept of
the ethical laws.   The first of these is the aforementioned golden
mean. In one of the most important par ts of the ethics, Aristotle
goes into the main virtues and vices, one by one, and shows how
there is a mean lying between them, and how this mean is almost
invariably preferable to either extreme.

Next he men tions the idea of justice.   Justice according
to Aristotle is a "correct relation between forces acting on and
acticated by, man." A just man is almost invariable a virtuous
on, and a life of virtuous activity, guided by reason and motivatd

Aristotle's Conception of the Source and Character of Ethical

Judgment as Opposed to that of Plato. With References to the

Dialogues.

Needless to say, such a subject as this cannot be considered in anything like entirety in such a short space. What we may
do however, is to outline the outstanding points of comparison,
and see how, in high light, the outstanding ideas of the two
great men are similar and how they are at odds.

To do this m we must consider the problem from three angles:
method of approach, the ultimate end in mind, and the actual
ethical code by which to reach your goal.

To begin with the Methods. As the high priest of dialectic,
Plato naturally builds his entire fabric around this "greatest
of all sciences". In the ethical problems which he considers
in the Symposium, and more particularly in the Philebus, Plato
invariably starts with a certain hypotheisis, and works back to
the elusive, and in most cases unattainable, first principls.
This must always be born in mind when studying Plato's methods.
He is always in search of a will-o-the-wisp immutable constant,
the essence of ethicalness. A goal which he himself is the first
to admit the difficulty of attainment and the impossiblity of
verbal or written explanation once the truth is seen. In this
sense Plato was a philosopher's philosopher. He was interested

ble of ultimately grasping the ultimate truths.

Aristotle admittedly in his ethics makes as great a up of
dialectic as anywhere in his writings. But even here his frown
of disapproval is apparent. He considers dialectic as the bas-
tard child of logic, to be used only when nothing else will suffie
The basis of the study is still the tried and true scientific
demonstration plan so completely outlined and explained in the
Organon. And the writing is shot through with Aristotle's in-
vairaible passion of categoriacal elimination. That is he is
confident that he could classify all possible alternitive, and
not only are all possible alternative available, but the final
truth can be idiscovered, expressed, and communicated.

The second main approach is to consider the end thatthe
two had in mind. Once again Plato is looking for the Ultimate
Priciple of Ethics, while Aristotle belie ves that a workable
code can be evolved, and that there is ,ina sense, no such thing
as the Ethics?of essence of Ethicalness. Always there is the
conflict between the abstract dialectical mentality of Plato,
and the down-to-earth, scientific procedure of Aristotle. Plaago
says, however, in the Symposium, that the object of ethi cs
should be, "To teach the sense of shame for what is base and
emulation for what is honorable anx fari." In this one in
stance at leawst, Plato says frankly what a practicla downto
earth objective for ethics could be.

find.

The remaining ethical necessity is the cultivation of the intellectual virtues. These are, scientific nowledge, natural intui-
tion, practical knowledge, and finally, if one was lucky,
wisdom. The cultivation of these is the highway to justice and to
virtue, and thence to the happiness the ulitmate end of all things
Aristotle believes moreover, that the prevailing standards for
good, evil, etc, are determined largely by the opinions of the intelligent thinking people of the time. Plato makes only one con
cession to this that ⊥ can find, which is when he says in the
Ph Symposium, "The good are a law unto themselves.

To sum up is difficult, but one may safely say, that both
men agree on the ultimate end of ethics, happiness, that they
probably disagree fundamentally on method and on the possibilkty t
of expressing the final truths, and that their respective codes of
eithics differ considerably, with Aristotle having the advantage
of specificty and clarity, and with Plato having the deeper
insght and the truer humanity.